Healthcare Chaplaincy

Pastoral Caregivers in the Medical Workplace

Written by Kathy J. Smith

Healthcare Chaplaincy

Pastoral Caregivers in the Medical Workplace

Written by Kathy J. Smith

ISBN 978-1-61529-191-5

Vision Publishing
P.O. Box 1680
Ramona, CA 92065
1 800-9-VISION
www.booksbyvision.org

All scripture is New American Standard unless otherwise stated.

Table of Contents

Foreword

Healthcare Chaplaincy is near and dear to my heart. In the year 2000, hospice care nurses and chaplains gave my family and I compassionate care during the loss of my first wife. More recently, chaplains spent many quality hours with my father, who recently passed. They provided a listening ear, prayers, and words of encouragement that were precious to my dad, easing him into eternity. Of course, their care did not end there. They continuously and compassionately listened to the concerns of my family during dad's transition.

Chaplains and their work are often under appreciated in the fast-paced work of modern medicine. Doctors, nurses, and other health care providers are not always cognizant of the psychological and spiritual needs of the patients in these areas, well trained chaplains are invaluable. Whether helping families deal with end of life issues, or the less traumatic but critical medical issues a patient faces, chaplains can often set the atmosphere for concerns of faith to be discussed. They can even facilitate a more rapid return to health and readjustment.

Kathy Smith as a registered nurse, chaplain, teacher, and writer has firsthand experience in all aspects of healthcare; hospital, nursing care, and hospice; and thus, she provides both the theory and the practical sides of chaplain care. This book, part of the Vision International University Chaplain Certificate Program is an excellent overview of this vital area of Christian ministry. If my wife and father were here today, they would be grateful to those that demonstrated the love of Christ to them. I too am grateful, and confident that this work will add the expertise needed to be even more effective as a Healthcare Chaplain.

Dr. Stan DeKoven

President and Founder Vision International University and Vision International Training and Education Network, Ramona, CA 92065

Introduction

Pure and undefiled religion in the sight of our God and Father is this: to visit orphans and widows in their distress, and to keep oneself unstained by the world. James 1:27

What is a chaplain? This is the question posed by one reporter to many different people in the street. He asked male and female, young and old. The answers were as varied as the people. One said, "Is that Charlie Chaplin?" Others either did not know or responded with a wide variety of different answers. A few of those answers included, minister, priest, member of the clergy, religious, preacher, a higher up, or someone who works for the church.

Perhaps the most notable response was given by a young man that appeared to be all of five years of age. He had the lengthiest and most profound definition of all. Part of what he said included, "someone who helps people when they are in surgery or want to talk to someone. They can be of any religion."[1]

So, for the purposes of this book, what is a chaplain? Chaplaincy might be considered a ministry of caregiving. More specifically, spiritual caregiving. It requires a passion to help people in need. People in prison, jail, hospice, nursing homes, or hospitals need spiritual guidance. In fact, we all need someone to support us when crisis strikes.

In the church, pastors provide spiritual guidance to individual members of their congregation. However, outside of the local church chaplains are often called upon to provide the needed spiritual support. Organizations such as police and fire departments often have a designated chaplain. The armed services or other government agencies may have a chaplain as well.

---

[1] Professional Chaplaincy, "What is a Chaplain?", link to video https://youtu.be/QcgBmQ13dec *

While pastors are usually church based and often connected to a specific denomination, chaplains are more commonly community based and minister to people of varying faiths, offering pastoral care to all who need it regardless of their religious or faith background. They provide guidance and support, often in times of illness, trauma, or other crises.

Theirs is a ministry of presence. They are available to listen with a heart of compassion and love. They offer godly counsel, prayer, and willingly share in the burden of grief and the joys of triumph.

In an extract from the book, The Work of the Chaplain, Paget and McCormack wrote:

> *"The ministry of presence is often undervalued. The sick wait for visitors, the lonely delight in company, and the fearful take comfort in companionship. The chaplain who is present— keeping watch—communicates God's assurance, "Fear not, for I am with you" (Isaiah 41:10, NKJV).*[2]

Those in a crisis may have no religious background at all, nevertheless, they do have a need. We know that as ambassadors of Christ it is our responsibility to be his hands and feet, caring for the sick, the widows, and those in prison.

> *"'Lord, when did we see You hungry, or thirsty, or a stranger, or naked, or sick, or in prison, and did not take care of You?' "Then He will answer them, saying, 'Truly I say to you, to the extent that you did not do it to one of the least of these, you did not do it to Me." Matthew 25:44b-45*

Chaplains who care for people in medical facilities have a unique role to play as a member of the patient's medical team. They must interact and coordinate their care with other health practitioners and caregivers, as well as with the patient's family.

---

[2]   https://www.regonline.com/custImages/330000/333184/TheWorkoftheChaplainExtract.pdf

Doctors, nurses, and other medical personnel provide care for the physical, emotional, or mental needs of patients. Spiritual needs may go unmet however, if no church representative or chaplain is available. Chaplains are now widely accepted as a member of the allied health team providing total patient care. In fact, "total patient care" is a phrase used by many medical facilities to designate the type of medical care they provide.

Total patient care as it relates to nursing is defined by having one primary nurse who manages the patient's plan of care; this maintains continuity and insures that all aspects of the individual patient's needs are met. One primary caregiver manages all nursing care; but treating the patient requires a full medical team. Often this team includes therapists, social workers, doctors, nurses, chaplains and potentially many others.

Kate Dudgeon of Continuum writes,

> *"Working in healthcare, I consistently encounter processes and care offerings that are very rigid and don't match up with the individual needs and values that patients have. Commonly, I hear stories about patients not feeling heard or respected by clinicians because what is recommended to them doesn't align with who they are and what they believe. A lot of these issues stem from the fact that, in medicine, people are traditionally triaged and cataloged by medical condition and/or need."[3]*

Planning for the care of patients in a medical crisis requires more than triage. Patients are not just another medical record, nor are they merely a disease or a diagnosis. Human beings are multi-faceted individuals with a soul, spirit, and a body. These three parts are interconnected and problems in one area affect the whole person.

---

[3] Drudgeon, Kate Understanding the Whole Patient, A Model for Holistic Patient Care June 2, 2015 of Continuum: https://www.continuuminnovation.com/en/how-we-think/blog/understanding-the-whole-patient

Holistic Care

Treating the disease or ailment is simply not enough; they are a whole person with feelings and needs. One primary need is respect. The patient needs to feel respected and valued. We must consider the needs of the whole person, not just the ailment. Therefore, a team approach is required so that the patient can reach optimum health and wellbeing. This is known as the holistic care approach.

Medical doctors do the physical assessment, order the tests, make a diagnosis, and order the corresponding treatment to correct the problem. The nurse or other clinical team members deliver the needed care as prescribed by the doctor; often the spiritual component of care is omitted. That is why a chaplain or another pastoral care giver is involved.

> *"As health care settings become more focused on patient experience and care for the whole person, issues of culture, diversity, personal beliefs, and values have come to the forefront. Staff are expected to deliver not only high-quality clinical care but to do so with compassion and care...As health care leaders and administrators face these challenges, unfortunately, many are unaware of a valuable resource that can contribute to their clinical care and organizational goals: professional chaplains."[4]*

Hospital chaplains or healthcare chaplains provide pastoral care to their constituents in the clinical setting. They are also known as workplace ministers. Unlike other members of the healthcare team, they may also maintain an active position in their faith community.

---

[4] Wintz, Rev. Sue How Chaplains Are A Valuable Part of the Health Care Team http://www.kevinmd.com/blog/2016/03/chaplains-valuable-part-health-care-team.html

"Most chaplains are also authoritative members of a faith community whose boundaries are not coterminous with health-care, ..." [5]

You may say chaplains maintain a foothold in both religious and medical environments. Chaplains play a vital role in bridging the gap between the patient's spiritual care and their physical care.

"In the United States, the chaplain is often regarded as the 'cultural broker' on the team (Joint Commission, 2006). As the cultural broker, the chaplain assists the patient, family and health-care team bridge any cultural, ethnic, or religious issue that may hinder communication between and among them. As experts in helping people identify and articulate their beliefs and values, chaplains have expertise in identifying and helping teams accommodate the cultural beliefs and practices families have." [6]

The chaplain must be a communication liaison that assesses the spiritual and cultural needs of the patient and their family; then successfully conveys these needs to the medical personnel on the interdisciplinary team. The chaplain then helps the medical team understand these needs to better accommodate them in their plan of care. As stated in the quote above, this makes them a "cultural broker".

As a retired nurse with experience in ICU, Open Heart, Step down Units, Med-Surg., Renal Dialysis, Home Health, nursing homes; as well as developing and training a Pastoral Care Team in a local church, I have had the unique opportunity to view spiritual caregiving from both sides of the fence. I understand the medical team and nursing staff and I see the patient from their perspective.

---

[5] Holst, Lawrence E., editor, Hospital Ministry--The Role of the Chaplain Today, Wipf & Stock Publishers of Eugene, Oregon 2006

[6] Cherny, Nathan; Fallon, Maria; Kassa, Stein; Portenoy, Russell; and Currow, David C.; authors, Oxford Textbook of Palliative Care 5th edition by Oxford University Press, United Kingdom 2015

As the former Director of Pastoral Care Ministry in a local church, I also understand the unique role a pastoral care provider can play on the medical team. Chaplains and Spiritual Care Givers help bridge the gap between the patient, family, and the medical personnel making holistic patient care not only possible, but a reality. Whole patient care or holistic care, consists of providing for the needs of the entire person; spirit, soul, and body.

The goal of *Healthcare Chaplaincy* is to help you, the reader, gain greater insight into the role of a spiritual care giver or chaplain. Specifically, we will focus on providing care within the healthcare system. Hospitals, nursing homes, rehab centers, and hospice, are just a few of the locations where healthcare chaplains are called upon to minister to those in need.

Two are better than one because they have a good return for their labor. For if either of them falls, the one will lift up his companion. But woe to the one who falls when there is not another to lift him up. Furthermore, if two lie down together they keep warm, but how can one be warm alone? And if one can overpower him who is alone, two can resist him. A cord of three strands is not quickly torn apart.

Ecclesiastes 4:9-12

Chapter One: The History and Biblical Foundation of Chaplaincy

"And if one member suffers, all the members suffer with it;"

1 Corinthians 12: 26a

We are all members of the same body, and as the scripture above indicates, we all hurt when one of our members hurts. Therefore, it is the responsibility of each member to support one another in times of need. However, some have a specific call to do this on a regular basis; to support those in need both inside and outside the body of Christ. The person called to this area of service is known as a chaplain.

A chaplain is an advocate or comforter that comes alongside those in need of support, offering godly assistance as one who bears with them the presence of the Lord. They are in fact acting as a physical paraclete. The term paraclete comes from the Greek word "parakletos" meaning advocate or comforter and can be found in the writings of John in the New Testament. The paraclete is a reference to the Holy Spirit. The word has roots from a word used in Job, referring to the "comforters" of Job.

Chaplains come alongside those who need assistance during times of great trial and distress. If we search for the biblical roots of the chaplain's ministry, we can begin in the book of Joshua. There the Levitical priests accompanied soldiers into battle, carrying the ark of the covenant. The ark of the covenant signified that God was with them, even during times of war. I am certain it must have brought those engaged in battle much peace, comfort, and encouragement. After all, if God be for you, who can be against you?

Again, in the New Testament book of Acts, the apostles addressed complaints that the widows were not being adequately provided for. Therefore, they appointed godly men to oversee their care and thereby released themselves to attend to prayer and study. The pastors of our present-day churches often find themselves in this same dilemma, too many people with needs and not enough hours in the day. It is for this reason that the ministry of chaplains, pastoral care teams, and other lay leaders is so essential.

Capella, Cloak of God's Presence

Many trace the origin of the chaplain ministry back to the early 4th century. The word 'chaplain' was derived from the Latin word 'capella' meaning cloak. A story frequently associated with this, is that of a gentleman from Tours named St. Martin. Born in what is now known as Hungary, he was a Roman soldier.

One day he ran across a very cold and destitute man begging. He wanted to help him, but he had no money to offer. He took off his own cloak and used his sword to slash it in half. He kept the first half for himself and covered the beggar with the second half.

That evening, he reportedly had a vision of Jesus wearing the half cloak. At that point, he surrendered his life to the Lord, was baptized in the church, and began his lifelong work. He was later named a patron Saint. Kings carried his capella into battle to signify that the presence of the Lord was with them.

The Capella

A cloak that signified the presence of the Lord.

It gave soldiers a sense of comfort and peace.

Today, chaplains are still carrying the presence of the Lord into trying and difficult situations; bringing comfort and peace to those in need. They offer a neutralizing of the drama filled emotional tension that surrounds people in crisis. Fear of the unknown can cause people to experience great anxiety, but the peace of God can bring a calmness even in the storm.

Many other biblical examples can be found in the depth of the scriptures. For instance, one of the most noteworthy stories is that of the "Good Samaritan" found in Luke 10:25-37. Jesus was asked by an expert in the law, "Who is my neighbor?"

> *"Jesus replied and said, "A man was going down from Jerusalem to Jericho, and fell among robbers, and they stripped him and beat him, and went away leaving him half dead. And by chance a priest was going down on that road, and when he saw him, he passed by on the other side. Likewise a Levite also, when he came to the place and saw him, passed by on the other side. But a Samaritan, who was on a journey, came upon him; and when he saw him, he felt compassion, and came to him and bandaged up his wounds, pouring oil and wine on them; and he put him on his own beast, and brought him to an inn and took care of him. On the next day he took out two denarii and gave them to the innkeeper and said, 'Take care of him; and whatever more you spend, when I return I will repay you.' Which of these three do you think proved to be a neighbor to the man who fell into the robbers' hands?" And he said, "The one who showed mercy toward him." Then Jesus said to him, "Go and do the same." Luke 10:25-37*

Our brother (neighbor) had need of assistance and the good Samaritan found it in his heart to provide the needed care despite cultural differences. He showed the love of God, mercy, and compassion through his actions. Jesus said, we should do likewise.

What about the care given by Ruth to her mother in law, Naomi? Or the care Jesus gave to the sick, deaf, paralyzed, blind, etc. Jesus was the greatest example of caregiving to the needs of mankind. We would do well to follow his example; bringing healing, comfort, and peace to those in need.

> *Blessed be the God and Father of our Lord Jesus Christ, the Father of mercies and God of all comfort who comforts us in all our affliction so that we will be able to comfort those who*

are in any affliction with the comfort with which we ourselves are comforted by God." 2 Corinthians 1:3-4.

Chaplains in Attendance of Nobles and Monarchs

History records chaplains in attendance in the homes of nobles and in historical monarchies.

"Castles with attached chaplains generally had at least one 'chapel', sometimes as grand as a cathedral...

Since in feudal times most laymen, for centuries even most noblemen, were poorly or not educated, the literate clergy was often employed as advisers and secretarial staff (as in a chancery) until the advent of legists and proper bureaucratic civil service (mainly under Absolutism), hence the term clerk, derived from Latin clericus ('clergyman'). This made them very influential in temporal affairs; there was also a moral impact since they heard the confessions of the elite."[7]

Governmental Chaplains

More recently in the United States, we can trace some of our own government's humble beginnings back to the first Continental Congress of 1774. There the congress chose to begin their meetings in prayer, and they appointed a pastor to do the honors. From that day to the present, our House of Representatives has chosen to appoint a chaplain to serve the House.

"The election of the Rev. William Linn as Chaplain of the House on May 1, 1789, continued the tradition established by the Continental Congresses of each day's proceedings opening with a prayer by a chaplain. The early chaplains alternated duties with their Senate counterparts on a weekly basis. The

---

[7] http://enterchaplains.blogspot.com/p/3000-year-history-of-chaplaincy.html

two conducted Sunday services for the Washington community in the House Chamber every other week. "[8]

In addition to opening the House sessions with prayer, the chaplain is also called upon to perform numerous other duties. They may need to officiate in weddings or funerals, schedule guest chaplains, or offer pastoral counseling.

Chaplains may serve in many different environments. We have the military, legislative bodies, jails and prisons, universities and colleges, in private clubs such as scouts, the Knights of Columbus, on ships, in private companies, and corporations. Police departments and fire departments often have a chaplain to assist and support them. There are many health care facilities such as hospitals, retirement homes, hospice, etc. that employ chaplains to serve their staff and patients.

Healthcare Chaplains

Chaplain history in medical facilities can only go back as far as such institutions have been in existence. Up until the turn of the 20th century, healthcare usually amounted to the care that could be delivered by the doctor making a house call.

Prior to that time, many of the sick were cared for privately at home or in almshouses that typically provided care for the destitute who were ill. In the United States in 1872 there were only 178 hospitals.

A six-bed ward (almshouse) was built in New York City in 1736, but a century later it evolved into Bellevue Hospital. In New Orleans, also in 1736, the predecessor of Charity Hospital was born. The Regional Hospital of Memphis, was established in 1860. It is the oldest hospital in Tennessee.

Public hospitals emerged in the United States in the years 1860 to 1930. Many were built by Catholic, Jewish, and Protestant

---

[8] http://chaplain.house.gov/chaplaincy/history.html

churches. Of course, the clergy of those organizations served in the spiritual support role. The chaplain, as a spiritual care giver and member of the medical team, did not exist in those early days. In fact, as the creation of our modern medical facilities have evolved, the administration of these facilities has become more secularly oriented.

> *"The first clinically trained chaplain to be appointed to a general hospital was Austin P. Guiles at Massachusetts General Hospital in 1930. In 1933, Russell Dicks succeeded Guiles as chaplain and CPE supervisor. Dicks was later employed at Presbyterian Hospital in Chicago, which was a member of the relatively young American Protestant Hospital Association (APHA)."* [9]

In the summer of 1942 Rev. Russell L. Dicks, the chaplain at Wesley Memorial Hospital of Chicago, expressed an interest in creating an organization for professional chaplains. He invited general hospital chaplains to meet with him at the 1946 annual meeting of the American Protestant Hospital Association(APHA). From this early meeting, an association for Protestant Hospital Chaplains was established.

Respect for the work of Rev. Dicks grew; the medical community appointed him to chair the APHA Commission to study religious work in hospitals. It was soon apparent that standards and certifications were needed. By 1950, standards had been adopted and the process of offering certification for chaplains had begun.

By the 1960's the inclusion of women in the certification process was initiated, and by the 1970's Catholic nuns were requesting certification. In the 1980's, the Commission for Hospital Accreditation had validated the standards of practice for hospital chaplains and hospitals felt obligated to begin offering spiritual care to their patients. The inclusion of chaplains among those that

---

[9]   http://www.professionalchaplains.org/files/professional_standards/standards_of_practice/standards_practice_professional_chaplains_acute_care.pdf

Medicare would reimburse contributed to the increased numbers of chaplains providing spiritual care in the healthcare industry. [10]

In 1971 another hospital, Lutheran General Hospital, commissioned a study to answer questions regarding the effectiveness of their pastoral care department. It identified the perceived role of spiritual care givers in the healing environment. The results of that study were published in a report titled, "Hospital Chaplains: Who Needs Them?" [11]

This study was repeated in 1981 and little change was found. Overall, the contribution of spiritual care givers in the healthcare environment was apparent and valued by patients and medical staff alike. However, the role of chaplains as members of the healthcare team was just beginning to evolve.

Initially, education of those involved in pastoral care in health based environments focused on two elements: developing empathetic relationships and listening/ counseling skills.

Demand for accountability in all health based services has fueled the evolving role of chaplains. Spiritual assessment and theological perspectives integrated with psychological skills and knowledge have changed the way spiritual care is delivered.

Diagnosis and care plan development are no longer relegated to the medical professionals, but are now tools of the pastoral care giver as well. Interest in the diagnostic aspects of spiritual care was heightened by the work of Paul Pruyser, in his book, *The Minister as Diagnostician (1976)*. He encouraged pastors to apply a theological perspective to the diagnosis of patient problems. Interestingly, he was not a pastor but a psychologist. More on this in chapter four on assessment.

---

[10] http://www.professionalchaplains.org/content.asp?contentid+31 A brief history of the Association of Professional Chaplains.

[11] https://docslide.net/documents/hospital-chaplains-who-needs-them.html

The Changing Role of Chaplains

The desire to focus on whole patient care rather than diagnosis based treatment, has been a contributing factor to the inclusion of chaplains on the healthcare team. The value of providing spiritual care along with medical care has affected the curriculum in medical schools as evidenced in the quote below:

> *"Several prominent organizations have recognized the importance of spiritual care. The Joint Commission on Accreditation of Healthcare Organizations has a policy that states: 'For many patients, pastoral care and other spiritual services are an integral part of health care and daily life. The hospital is able to provide for pastoral care and other spiritual services for patients who request them.'"*[12]

In this same article by Christina M. Puchalski, MD, MS also stated:

> *"Technology has led to phenomenal advances in medicine and has given us the ability to prolong life. However, in the past few decades, physicians have attempted to balance their care by reclaiming medicine's more spiritual roots, recognizing that until modern times spirituality was often linked with health care. Spiritual or compassionate care involves serving the whole person—the physical, emotional, social, and spiritual. Such service is inherently a spiritual activity"*

The Body, Soul, and Spirit Connection to Healthcare

The move to treat the whole patient has created a renewed interest in spiritual care giving as an integral part of the overall wellness plan in modern day medical facilities. That said, most of our medical clinicians recognize their own shortcomings in providing

---

[12] Puchalski, Christina M.; MD, MS; author The Role of Spirituality in Health Care. https://www.ncbi.nlm.nih.gov/pmc/articles/PMC1305900/

such care. Therefore, an increased need for the assistance of chaplains on the interdisciplinary medical team is being recognized and valued.

In Viktor Frankl's words,

"No cure that fails to engage our spirit
can make us well"[13]

Caring for the whole patient is paramount in providing an optimum resolution to health care challenges. Therefore, the future of health care chaplaincy would seem to be growing and expanding in the 21st century. Now acceptance of Chaplains on the interdisciplinary team is gaining momentum as an integral part of providing whole patient care.

Conclusion

The global history of chaplains engaged in military and legislative roles dates to the 4th century; while healthcare chaplaincy in the United States is a comparatively recent development. Nevertheless, the role of chaplains and their acceptance in the healthcare arena is opening new doors of opportunity for those who hear the call. No longer a mere opportunity to listen and pray for the needs of patients, the evolving role of chaplains has grown to include many different facets of spiritual care and counseling.

---

[13] http://www.professionalchaplains.org/store_product.asp?prodid=31

Chapter One Questions

1. What are some of the biblical roots of chaplaincy that the author identified in this text?

2. What does the word "capella" mean and what does it have to do with the history of chaplaincy?

3. When did chaplains first appear in their role in our US government?

4. How did the change in healthcare practice to focus on whole patient care affect the role of chaplains in our medical facilities?

Chapter Two: What is a Healthcare Chaplain?

"Chaplaincy is being there for people in their darkest times. When they need somebody the most, when a lot of people aren't there for them."

Beth Gilbert, Chaplain LLU Medical Center[14]

The hospital bed can be one of the loneliest places in the world. Medical staff are often overworked and family may be unavailable to meet the emotional and spiritual needs of a patient in crisis. Even in medical institutions outside of the hospital, you will find people in need of guidance and the listening ear that a chaplain can provide. They are there to give vital care in some of life's most critical circumstances

Chaplains are uniquely equipped to support the patient's belief systems regardless of their faith or culture. When big questions come up such as, why did this happen to me? Or where is God in this chaos, doesn't God care? Chaplains are available to offer spiritual guidance.

They know how to navigate through the healthcare experience and act as knowledgeable guides insuring the needs of the patient and their families are met. As members of the interdisciplinary medical team, they serve as advocates insuring the spiritual concerns of the patient are included in the daily plan of care. They may be there to collaborate with the whole medical team during morning rounds.

---

[14] https://youtu.be/zrCditxjyTA   Video Career Profiles - Chaplain by LomaLinda 360

A Day in the Life of a Chaplain

A typical day in the life of a hospital chaplain may begin early with pre-round activities; preparing both in mind and spirit by reviewing patient records of all needing assistance during their day. It may include meeting with other professional chaplains for a time of prayer and devotions, gearing up for whatever circumstances they may encounter.

Often the next step is interacting with the hospital staff, hearing about their concerns and needs. This may include personal needs as well as the patient's needs. Chaplains do not care only for the patients, they also provide spiritual care and support to the medical team of which they are integral members.

I remember, during my years working as a nurse in the hospital, the frustration of trying to care for the whole patient; body, soul, and spirit. Time to meet all their needs and the needs of their families was often lacking. I did not lack in desire to help, just in the time to provide it.

Medical personnel who are responsible for the care of multiple patients often find it difficult to carve out time to hear the concerns and fears of their patients and their families. Even if they have the time to listen, many feel ill equipped to provide the spiritual care and guidance that is needed.

Let's face it, in the interest of saving money, often hospital personnel are maxed out with patient loads that are far too demanding. This makes essential physical care all they have time to perform. It is not that they do not want to take time to listen, they simply do not <u>have</u> the time. Tie that to the ever-present crisis that becomes a part of the medical facilities' norm, and you have less than optimal patient care.

Chaplains Serve as a Bridge

In recent years, chaplains have been identified as an important member of the medical team. They bridge the growing gap by providing a listening ear and spiritual guidance. They facilitate better communication between medical personnel and their patients, becoming an active advocate for both parties. A patient's satisfaction with their personal medical care can be greatly enhanced when a chaplain becomes actively involved.

According to Healthcare Chaplaincy,

> *"Professional health care chaplains help anyone whatever their beliefs, values, or culture to find meaning and comfort when dealing with a life-changing health situation. They're one of the most cost-effective resources to increase patient, family, and staff satisfaction".[15]*

A healthcare chaplain may be board certified by one of many professional associations when he or she meets the requirements of that specific board. Some professional chaplains may also be ordained clergy or recognized as religious/spiritual leaders depending on their tradition; some are not.

Local churches may also develop teams of people who provide pastoral care to those directly connected to their constituents, their families, and associates who are institution or homebound due to illness; including physical, mental, or emotional issues. These teams may be collectively named as pastoral care teams, or home care teams, or another title as determined by the religious body they represent. While local clergy and religious leaders may volunteer to see patients in healthcare facilities, they are free to serve only patients of their own religious faith if that is what they wish.

---

[15]Healthcare Chaplaincy; "Professional Chaplains Role"; https://youtu.be/Ox3NpIKyAPI

Other professional healthcare chaplains, such as those found in hospitals or hospice facilities, usually care for people of various religious backgrounds no matter what faith they profess. They provide for the spiritual care of patients and their families across the board regardless of their beliefs.

Workplace Ministers

Healthcare chaplains provide pastoral care to people within the healthcare system; first to the patients and their families and secondly to the medical staff. Essentially, chaplains are workplace ministers. Their medical workplace may include hospice, homecare, medical or surgical facilities, long term care, rehab centers, palliative care, or homes for the mentally challenged.

They may minister to a wide range of age, ethnic, and culturally diverse people groups. They could minister to children and their families in an acute care facility such as a children's hospital; or in a hospice or burn unit that focuses on patients under eighteen years of age. Or at the opposite end of the spectrum, they may deal with people in retirement or acute care facilities that are dealing with end of life concerns. Lastly, they help all age and ethnic groups in between the two extremes.

A health care chaplain is often fully certified and ordained. This minister has chosen to focus on those who are dealing with injury, illness, or other health related crises. A pastor shepherds the flock in his own congregation, but a healthcare chaplain is a pastor to those within the healthcare system.

Some of the duties that a chaplain may be called upon to perform are counseling the patient and/or family, helping patients work through anger or grief, or even sitting with those who are dying. We will discuss this in much greater detail later in this book.

Rev. Sue Wintz of Health Care Chaplaincy Network writes,

> *"Professional chaplains have been part of hospitals and other health care settings for decades: spiritual care specialists who*

contribute a unique expertise to interdisciplinary teams....
They bring expertise that is essential to patient and family
care, including: assessing, responding, documenting, and
communicating issues of spiritual distress and interventions to
other members of the team..."[16]

Please note that the qualifications for chaplains vary from one
facility to another and from one religious institution to another.
Experience in a leadership role within a church environment is
usually mandatory. Some organizations insist on two to four years
of leadership experience and many require ordination; however,
this can vary from one organization to another.

Christie Shine Chaplain LLU Medical Center comments that "The
hardest part of being a chaplain is heartache, it can be very sad to
be there to work with people in times of trauma."[17]

Another chaplain, Jim Greek, D Min., LLU Medical Center recalls
being home with his own eight-year-old son, when he got the call
to come to the hospital. This man was crying in the corner with his
son, his son was also eight years old.

The little boy had asked his father to play ball but the father told
him he did not have the time, so the little boy went to the backyard
to play by himself. There was a stream behind the house and the
little boy fell in and drowned. The father was there in the hospital
just yelling, "I'm ready to play ball now. I'm ready to play ball."

This situation hit so very close to home, except by the grace of God
we could be walking in this father's shoes. The chaplain goes on to

---

[16] Wintz, Rev. Sue, author; http://www.kevinmd.com/blog/2016/03/chaplains-valuable-part-health-care-team.html

[17] https://youtu.be/zrCditxjyTA Video Career Profiles - Chaplain by LomaLinda 360

relate, "Often you can get really attached to people's journeys. All you can do is to be there to help in their time of need."[18]

Personal Qualities of a Chaplain

What are the gifts and talents that a chaplain needs to possess? There are many to be certain; a caring heart, a listening ear, a compassionate spirit, and an astute sensitivity to others. It is someone that can offer godly advice without becoming judgmental or critical, and at times, long suffering. Perhaps some of the best fruit one can bear in the ministry of caregiving are those of the Spirit found in Galatians 5:22-23. They are love, joy, peace, patience, kindness, goodness, faithfulness, gentleness, and self-control.

It is the responsibility of the chaplain to bring with them the presence of God, creating a haven of peace even in the middle of life's storms. The caregiver becomes a "paraclete" that comes alongside the patient and the family and offers support and strength. It requires knowing how to be a catalyst to calm the storm even when tension and anxiety are high and hope seems lost. Chaplains become the anchor of hope that keeps others afloat even in a sea of despair.

The chaplain must possess a thick skin but be gentle of heart. One who can empathize and hear their fears and concerns, whether imaginary or real. These concerns are real to the patient. The chaplain must be willing to listen; offering prayer, scripture, and practical guidance as is appropriate in each individual case. Each one will be unique. Each one will have differing needs and expectations.

The chaplain needs to be an astute observer of human behavior; discerning more than the words and behavior expressed and able to peer into the heart to understand the real issues as they present

---

[18] https://youtu.be/zrCditxjyTA video Career Profiles - Chaplain by LomaLinda 360

themselves. Dealing one by one with the concerns of the patient and offering hope, even if the only hope they can offer is a peaceful transition and consolation to those they leave behind.

Chaplains must pour out of their abundance from within, ministering with the same spirit that they have been filled with themselves. Therefore, they must remain rested and fresh, well prepared in prayer and in study of the word. One cannot pour out of an empty vessel. Periodic times of refreshing and refilling are necessary, for without it the chaplain becomes vulnerable to the hopelessness and despair that many patients experience.

While the term chaplain may not appear in your bible, we can look to the book of Titus for some general qualifications outlined by Paul for those in church leadership.

Titus 1:5-9,

" For this reason I left you in Crete, that you would set in order what remains and appoint elders in every city as I directed you, namely if any man is above reproach, the husband of one wife, having children who believe, not accused of dissipation or rebellion. For the overseer must be above reproach as God's steward, not self-willed, not quick-tempered, not addicted to wine, not pugnacious, not fond of sordid gain, but hospitable, loving what is good, sensible, just, devout, self-controlled, holding fast the faithful word which is in accordance with the teaching, so that he will be able both to exhort in sound doctrine and to refute those who contradict." (also see Timothy 3:1-13).

Peter weighs in below:

"Therefore, I exhort the elders among you, as your fellow elder and witness of the sufferings of Christ, and a partaker also of the glory that is to be revealed, shepherd the flock of God among you, exercising oversight not under compulsion, but voluntarily, according to the will of God; and not for sordid gain, but with eagerness; nor yet as lording it over those

allotted to your charge, but proving to be examples to the flock. And when the Chief Shepherd appears, you will receive the unfading crown of glory."1 Peter 5:1-4

So Why Become a Chaplain?

Chaplains express a sense of satisfaction and purpose while fulfilling their role in the healthcare workplace. They have the opportunity to walk out a portion of life's journey with someone in need, improving the lives of their patients and their families. Most consider it a calling with an eternal reward.

They have a pastor's heart, but their congregation is found in the healthcare world, rather than a church. They provide crucial spiritual care by determining the patient's needs through observation, prayer, and a professional assessment. Next, they develop a plan to help them work through the difficulties and find resolution. The patient's need determines the care; the chaplain merely guides the patient as they walk through the process.

At times, it may only require listening to the patient's concerns and allowing them to vent their frustrations and anger. Other times, there may be some real issues that need to be resolved, and the chaplain helps steer them through the process of resolution. When end of life is inevitable, the chaplain helps the patient and family work through the stages of grief to acceptance.[19]

Chaplains find very creative ways to help their patients and bring acceptance of their diagnosis and prognosis. For instance, one young mother relates how the chaplains helped her dying husband record information he wanted to share with his small daughter. Now that he has passed on and the daughter is growing up, she is able to hear those things he wanted to share with her via video recordings. He is still sowing into her life long after he went on to

---

[19] DeKoven, Stan E. Ph.D. author; Grief Relief; Vision Publishing, Ramona, CA 978-1931178860 http://www.booksbyvision.org

be with the Lord; all because the chaplains helped him preserve his legacy.

Another chaplain relates how he discovered his dying patient had a gift for art. The chaplain's hospice organization arranged to have his work mounted and enlisted the assistance of an art gallery to display the paintings during a special event. The patient and his family were grateful that the paintings were celebrated while he was still alive to take part in the gallery's open house.

Chaplains make a difference in the lives of their patients, their families, and the faculty at the healthcare facility where they work. Most do not do what they do for the monetary reward, but for the eternal. This coupled with personal satisfaction and sense of fulfillment drives them to help others and fulfill their calling as a healthcare chaplain.

Chapter Two Questions

1. How do chaplains bridge the communication gap between medical staff and the patients and their families?

2. What is meant by the term "workplace minister"?

3. What personal qualities do you think are most desirable for a chaplain to possess and why?

4. Why do you want to become a chaplain?

Chapter Three: Chaplains as a Member of the Interdisciplinary Medical Team

In their special report on Hospital Chaplains, ABC TV news (2012) followed Chaplain Di Roche on her rounds in the Intensive Care unit of Royal North Shore hospital. Di is a non-denominational chaplain who works exclusively with critically ill patients and their families in Sydney, Australia.

Head of the ICU of the Royal North Shore Hospital, Dr. Ray Raper, shared with the reporter that he has a keen sense of responsibility to look out for the broader interests of his patients, which includes the patient's family. He stated that Chaplain Di plays a significant role in providing the needed support for the families in their time of crisis. Obviously, Chaplain Di is a valued member of the interdisciplinary medical team of the ICU. [20]

Define Interdisciplinary Team

What is an Interdisciplinary medical team? What are the titles, roles, and functions of its members? How does the chaplain interact with the rest of the team? These important questions must be answered to gain a full understanding of how the chaplain fulfills his or her role.

According to the Free Dictionary:

> *"An interdisciplinary team is a group of health care professionals from diverse fields who work in a coordinated fashion toward a common goal for the patient."*[21]

The patient's health and well-being <u>are</u> the common goal of the team. The professionals must find a way to coordinate their plans

---

[20] http://youtu.be/rwC_wgwgxXE

[21] http://medical-dictionary.thefreedictionary.com/interdisciplinary+team

for the patient's care. Without the team members talking and collaborating with one another, they could end up with conflicting plans and disjointed care.

Let me explain what I mean. Think about a football team and how they work together. They have numerous players all with the same goal. Their objective is to get the ball across the goal line. Left to their own with no strategy or plan, the team's actions would lack cohesiveness and their efforts would be uncoordinated. Without good communication and a willingness of team members to work together, their efforts could become a chaotic mess, with minimal or no success.

Who are the Members on the Team?

Most patients have numerous professionals working together on their team. Although this is not a complete list, the team may include some or all the following: Registered nurses, doctors, nursing assistants, LVN/LPN, dietician, radiologist, physical therapist, occupational therapist, dietician, phlebotomist, respiratory therapist, social worker, psychologist, psychiatrist, and yes, the chaplain.

In the interdisciplinary approach to healthcare, each team member contributes their own expertise and knowledge to the plan of care for the patient. Understanding the role each member plays and the scope of their practice is important to the overall success of this collaboration. Providing optimal support and care to the patient is the overarching goal of this approach to patient care. The team understands that treating the whole person rather than the ailment is imperative.

Advancements in the Practice of Medicine

"The Joint Commission on the Accreditation of Healthcare Organizations (JCAHO, 1998) in the U.S. states, "Patients have a fundamental right to considerate care that safeguards

their personal dignity and respects their cultural, psychosocial, and spiritual values.[22]

The hospital accrediting organization known worldwide as JCAHO, acknowledged the need for whole patient care back in 1998. Since then, the trend toward treating the whole person rather than just a diagnosis has become the standard for modern medical practice. The patient is more than appendicitis, or a tonsillectomy. The patient is more than the medical record number identifying them on their chart. They are human beings with feelings and concerns that affect the overall success of their care.

Terms such as holistic medicine or integrated health care are also used in conjunction with this evolving approach to modern day healthcare. The result of this transition to whole patient care, is a healthcare system that recognizes the need to consider all aspects of the patient's needs and care, not just the physical component. A human being is three parts: body, soul, and spirit as stated before. If there is a problem in one area it affects all three.

What Roles Do Other Team Members Play?

It is for this reason that the interdisciplinary team may include a multitude of professions such as psychiatrists, psychologists, and chaplains along with all the rest of the medical personnel. The goal is to treat the whole person, not just part. So how does such a potentially large team interact with one another without over-lapping or overriding one another's care?

The nurse is the hub of the communication wheel, managing patient cares and concerns as their advocate. They monitor the vitals, assess patient needs, and manage personal care. The nurse is the patient's voice. When a critical abnormality appears, the nurse reports it to the proper personnel and follows through as is appropriate until the problem is resolved.

---

[22]   https://www.healthcarechaplaincy.org/userimages/professional-chaplaincy-its-role-and-importance-in-healthcare.pdf page 82

For instance, if the patient suddenly spikes a high temperature or the blood pressure drops dangerously low; the nurse uses his/her nursing judgement to administer any medication on the patient's orders that will correct the situation. If the nurse does not have standing orders for a medication that will correct the problem, then the appropriate physician is notified to get orders that will resolve the problem.

Likewise, if the nurse notices the patient is not eating well, he or she will bring it to the attention of the primary care physician or even suggest a visit from the dietician on staff. The nurse manages and coordinates the patient care within the scope of the doctor's orders.

In addition to the primary care physician and nursing personnel, a social worker/case manager may be assigned to the patient's team. Often the social worker assists by making the arrangements for needed care to transition from the skilled care setting to a home, rehab, or other long-term facility. They help develop a discharge plan and identify the appropriate support services.

They may assist a victim of domestic violence find a shelter, or help with placement of the elderly in assisted living facilities. They may help the patient apply for government assistance such as WIC, food stamps, disability benefits, or Medicare. They also locate needed services such as meals on wheels, or transportation services as are appropriate for the patient. The social worker's role may include patient counselor, advocate, educator, or mediator.

Most know the role that the physical therapist plays in helping to restore strength, flexibility, mobility, and physical function. An occupational therapist on the other hand helps restore and improve performance of activities needed for daily living. For instance, learning how to button a shirt or tie your shoes after experiencing a stroke or paralysis that limits the use of one's arm. Occupational therapists teach patients how to compensate for their handicaps, whether temporary or permanent, allowing them to perform the skills needed for everyday living.

Respiratory therapists may be called upon to administer breathing treatments or manage oxygen levels of patients with compromised respiratory systems. There are many specialties that could become a part of the patient's interdisciplinary team. Time and space do not allow us to go into detail for each one in this book.

Each member of the team involved with the patient's care will do their own initial assessment of the patient's condition. The nurse will do a nursing assessment and develop a nursing plan of care. The doctor does his assessment and writes his orders for treatments, care, diet, and medication. He may choose to request the assistance of other specialists as well.

At times, the team may need to meet with one another to discuss the patient's needs, offer insights into care, and coordinate how the goals for care will be met. The primary concern for you, the reader, is to know the role of the chaplain and how to interact with the rest of the team.

According to Sue Wintz (HCCN), director, professional and community education, there are several steps that every healthcare leader should take now.

"The first step is determining whether your organization has a chaplain(s) on the team. If not, an essential element of whole-person care is missing.

Next, ensure that the chaplain has the education, training and credentialing that is recognized within the profession, and advocate for competency for best patient outcomes.

Encourage other members of the interdisciplinary team to obtain basic knowledge of spiritual care to incorporate into their scope of practice and to facilitate interactions with and referrals to chaplains."[23]

---

[23] Wentz, Rev. Sue; Director, professional and community education of HCCN, author; http://www.kevinmd.com/blog/2016/03/chaplains-valuable-part-health-care-team.html

The Role of Chaplains on the Team

The chaplain's role on the interdisciplinary team is to assess the patient's spiritual needs and develop a care plan to meet those needs. The spiritual care plan that the chaplain develops may or may not affect the rest of the medical staff. Remember that much of the care provided by the chaplain will be driven from the patient's need. Patients may need little more than someone to listen. At other times, they may need you, as their chaplain, to guide them through the process of denial, anger, bargaining, depression, and acceptance.

Others may have real concerns about their spiritual life and may ask some very difficult questions. As Chaplain, you may not know the answers to all their questions and that is okay. Be honest and get the answers to their questions and get back with them. The initial visit to a patient's room is to offer a listening ear and express genuine concern for the patient and their family.

Introducing yourself as the chaplain and developing a connection to the patient is the first step. Inquiring about the patient's reason for being there, their family, and their personal needs and concerns will reinforce that you are genuinely concerned. If you will be yourself and allow yourself to be transparent they will begin to value and trust you. Trust is the key to creating valuable pastoral relationships with the patients, relationships that may be trans-formational.

While the role of the chaplain is to provide spiritual care to the patient, patient's family, and the medical staff; the responsibilities of the chaplain may be varied as determined by the facility employing the chaplain and their expectations. A partial list of potential responsibilities may include:

1. Conducting religious ceremonies such as funerals, baptisms, and marriages. Providing communion to those who request it.

2. Providing grief counseling, marriage therapy, addiction and crisis interventions, group therapy.
3. Participating in education and training.
4. Coordinating activities of volunteers and clergy from the community.
5. Performing chapel services for patients and their family.

Conclusion

Chaplains have a unique role as members of the medical team, but unlike their fellow teammates, they have a responsibility to both the medical and spiritual communities. They make themselves accountable to the caregivers on their medical team, but the care they give is spiritually based. It can be challenging at times, but comes with eternal rewards.

Chapter Three Questions

1. What is your definition of an interdisciplinary team?

2. Name two members of the interdisciplinary team (not including chaplain) and their roles.

3. What is the role of the chaplain on the interdisciplinary team? What contribution may the chaplain have to offer other professionals on this team?

4. What are some of the responsibilities a chaplain may be called upon to perform?

Chapter Four: Assessment and The Care Plan

Much of the work of earlier chaplains was limited to listening, praying, and the reading of scripture. They had the authority to do ministerial work with the sick as stated above, but were not encouraged to add to their repertoire the skills of assessment, evaluation, and treatment.

Diagnosis and Ministry

Paul Pruyser, a clinical psychologist at the Menninger Foundation, played a key role in changing the framework from which pastoral care in the medical setting was practiced. His own theological insights, seminary consultations and teaching experiences, as well as his close relationships with ministers afforded him the opportunity to influence the educational preparation of ministers for such work. He went on to author the book (1976), *"The Minister as Diagnostician."*

The question he posed was simple, what if the minister could assess, diagnose, and treat the spiritual problems of the patient? Furthermore, why shouldn't he? Who is better equipped to treat the spiritual maladies affecting the patient and possibly the patient's health? The physician was trained to treat the physical body, so why not allow the chaplain the opportunity to treat the spiritual body?

Much of Pruyser's work was by his own admission, heavily influenced by his colleague and predecessor, Thomas W. Klink. Klink penned many articles on pastoral psychology and the involvement of pastoral clinicians in the care of patients. He and Pruyser did much to acknowledge and give credibility to the diagnostic and treatment abilities of pastoral caregivers. They both felt that because of the pastoral caregiver's theological knowledge and experience, the potential for insightful spiritual assessment, evaluation, and treatment could add a dimension to the interdisciplinary team that no one else could provide.

The contribution of chaplains to whole patient care made them a valid and valuable resource to the whole medical team. The modern-day role of chaplains has become a marriage in thought between theology and psychology.

Paul Pruyser was of the mindset that if theology taught in seminary was good, theology and sociology together were better, but theology, sociology, and psychology were best. Each adds a layer of knowledge and perspective that helps one see the problem and subsequent solution more fully. The result is better care and resolution for the patient.

He became frustrated with theologians borrowing terminology from psychological diagnosis rather than having their own diagnostic terminology with which to interact with the other disciplines on the team. It was out of this frustration that he birthed a set of seven guidelines for pastoral diagnosis that are still referenced today.

They were:

1. Awareness of the Holy
2. Providence
3. Faith
4. Grace or gratefulness
5. Repentance
6. Communion
7. Sense of Vocation[24]

While it is important to understand how these early models for spiritual assessment began, we will not elaborate on his thesis further within the confines of this book. If you would like to

---

[24] Pruyser, Paul W.; author; The Minister as Diagnostician, ISBN 0-664-24123-9 published by The Westminster Press, 1976.

review his entire concept, it is outlined in detail in chapter 5 of his book.

Worthy to be noted here is the work of George Fitchett[25]. In his book, "Assessing Spiritual Needs", he lays out a framework for assessing spiritual needs in an approach he titled, 7 x 7. He prefers to use seven holistic and seven spiritual dimensions as bench-marks.

Others who have made significant contributions to the evolving process of spiritual assessment are Dr. Elizabeth McSherry and Mark LaRocca-Pitts BBC. Dr. McSherry has challenged chaplains to submit their assessment to an empirical test using more of a scientific approach to assessing patient data.

In Chaplaincy Today[26], Mark LaRocca-Pitts BCC writes about his three "distinctions" in spiritual assessment. They are: spiritual screens, spiritual histories, and spiritual assessments. He identifies spiritual screens as the most basic of the three. Spiritual screening is the acquiring of basic information regarding denomination or cultural affiliation of the patient's faith. This is often obtained during the admission process by the nurse or admission technician.

The second category is the spiritual history. It includes how the patient's faith impacts their medical care. Regardless of how the patient expresses and practices their faith, the chaplain shows respect for those beliefs. The chaplain is there in a supportive role only. It is not permissible to use this opportunity to convert the patient's faith practices. If the chaplain feels uncomfortable or inadequate to act in a supportive role, then a referral is appropriate in such cases.

---

[25] Fitchett, George Assessing Spiritual Needs, A Guide for caregivers, 0-7880-9940-x published by Academic Renewal Press, Lima, Ohio 2002

[26] Chaplaincy Today e-Journal of the Association of Professional Chaplains Volume 28 Number 1 Spring/Summer 2012

Finally, there is the category of spiritual assessment. This is a much more in-depth look at the patient's spiritual history. The purpose of this detailed exploration is to identify areas of potential concern and to determine an appropriate intervention and develop a subsequent plan of care.

Many others have gone on to develop their own framework upon which to assess the needs of patients and their families. We have done the same and will review in detail later in this chapter.

Patient Visits

Chaplains in a healthcare setting may provide patients one or more visits. The first visit may be initiated by a referral of the medical staff for a specific need, or take place during routine rounds. The number of visits a chaplain provides to any one patient is determined by the needs of the patient, their family, and the length of their stay.

The goal of the initial visit is not only to become acquainted with the patient and their family, but also to acquire the basic history needed to complete a preliminary assessment of the patient's needs. In the terms outlined by LaRocca-Pitts, this would be spiritual screening. It is the briefest and least invasive form of spiritual assessment.

What is Assessment?

For some patients, one visit is all the chaplain will have time to fit in before the patient is discharged. Acute observation skills and keen spiritual discernment are helpful in determining the need for further assessment.

What is assessment? In his book, *Assessment in Counseling*,[27] Dr. Stan DeKoven defines it like this:

---

[27] DeKoven, Stan E. Ph.D. author; Assessment in Counseling; Vision Publishing, Ramona, CA August 2010 978-1-61529-0-055; page 10. http://www.booksby vision.org/product/assessment-in-counseling/

"Assessment is nothing more than the gathering of facts, information that, when skillfully combined into a coherent whole can provide a clear picture of an individual, circumstance or situation. In the field of counseling, assessment is the utilization of the manmade and God given (yourself, His gifts) tools to arrive at a diagnosis of the problem(s) of a person or family, so intervention or treatment can begin."

I found his definition of what assessment is not to be equally as important: I quote:

"Assessment of needs, though vital in terms of insight and understanding of individual needs or differences, is not a substitute for compassion, clinical skill, or integrity. Each tool that you will learn to use is but one piece of information about a member of God's precious creation. Humans are wonderfully complex, and truly the whole person is greater than the sum of the parts that we gather in our assessment process."[28]

In his book, *Assessing Spiritual Needs*, George Fitchett defines assessment as both process and perception. In other words, assessment includes the process of gathering adequate information to determine the patient's condition and needs, but it is also a perception and interpretation of the meaning of the information gathered. It may include objective and subjective observations and known data.

For instance, an assessment may include facts such as medical diagnosis, the circumstances that initiated the patient visit, family, and personal history. Assessment should also include observations of the patient and family, it is especially important to document anything that is outside of the accepted norm.

If the patient does not demonstrate or vocalize any signs or symptoms of concern, it is equally important to document that as

---

[28] DeKoven, Stan E. Ph.D. author; Assessment in Counseling; Vision Publishing, Ramona, CA August 2010 978-1-61529-0-055; page 10. http://www.booksby vision.org/product/assessment-in-counseling/

well. Any subjective conclusions you come to need to be supported by the objective information that led you to that conclusion.

When documenting the patient is adjusting to hospital environment without difficulty, you need to supply the observations that led you to that conclusion. You may write that the patient appears relaxed, smiles easily, and is friendly and communicative. Family interacts with patient in providing care and emotional support. Then go on to describe what the family did to provide this support. Staff reports the patient is cooperative with care. Utilize all your senses, physical, emotional, mental, and spiritual, to discern problems and concerns. What did you see, hear, feel, smell, or sense?

An assessment that uncovers potential problems needs to be documented thoroughly in detail. For instance, a female patient presents with a broken jaw. Her male friend answers questions for her explaining she fell down the steps when getting up to get a drink in the middle of the night. The female becomes noticeably apprehensive whenever he approaches her. Attempts to have the patient speak for herself are met with resistance from the male. The female does not make eye contact with staff and answers questions with one or two words, offering no additional information.

One would want to record every detail observed both subjective and objective. Previous history of unusual injuries, history of domestic violence, and any other pertinent data need to be well documented before an appropriate intervention can be determined. Assessment is both process and perception.

Perception is what you sensed, felt, and observed. Process, how did you process this information and to what conclusions does it lead you? The conclusion would be your spiritual diagnosis. With each diagnosis, we must also address the need for an appropriate goal and intervention. What interventions would be most appropriate for the stated diagnosis?

As a nurse, I learned assessment skills in school as it related to the needs of the whole patient, hence the term whole patient care. Admitting a patient to a medical facility began with an extensive admission interview. In depth questions were asked and the answers documented regarding the patient's physiological, psychological, sociological, and spiritual status.

Based upon the information gathered in this interview, the nurse would develop a nursing care plan to provide for the patient's needs and address their problems within the scope of practice. For instance, the patient may have dietary restrictions based upon religious practices or cultural influences. In some cases, the family may refuse certain treatments such as blood transfusions based upon their religious beliefs. All such information is of vital importance.

Protocol and Legal Concerns

While much of the information documented in the patient's chart may be helpful to the chaplain in preparing for the first visit, not all medical facilities allow chaplains access to this information. Limited or no access is often the case for volunteer chaplains or others not employed by the facility where the patient is admitted.

It is important to know the rules and regulations of the facility where your patient is admitted. Compliance with the regulations of the facility are vital to protect both yourself and the medical facility. No one wants to be slapped with a violation of the HIPAA Act. That could be costly, cumbersome, and could even jeopardize your future as a chaplain.

Since the Health Information Portability and Accountability Act (HIPAA) was enacted on August 21, 1996, medical professionals and medical facilities alike must monitor their own compliance carefully. Violations of this act would be a serious matter for all concerned and compliance is mandatory.

While not all information contained in the medical chart is of significance to the chaplain, an overview of the content is helpful when access to the patient record is possible. Understanding why the patient was admitted, the prognosis and medical care plan, as well as any social and spiritual history will be beneficial.

Getting an overview of the patient before the initial visit will better prepare the chaplain for any issues that may need to be addressed. If access to the medical record is not possible, asking medical staff about any concerns they wish to make you aware of could be helpful as well.

The Initial Visit

The first time a chaplain meets the patient or the patients' family, they begin with the customary introductions. Ask the patient and or family to tell you about themselves and what brought them to the facility. Try to get a sense of the family dynamics and any existing support system.

Ask about any problems, concerns, or prayer requests. Use open ended questions to help draw out the patient and their family but avoid prying. Show an interest in, and respect for, the patient's individual faith journey. Find ways to come alongside them to encourage and support them on their chosen path.

Be transparent and honest; you will want to begin building a trusting relationship on the initial visit. Respect for the individual and protection of the patient's confidentiality are key. As the patient's confidence in you grows, they will be more willing to share openly their thoughts and concerns.

At times, the patient will merely need someone to listen, just having someone to vent to can be comforting. Other times, they will have more pressing needs that need to be addressed. Always ask permission to pray for them, or if appropriate, read them a scripture.

Your intervention may end here if the patient is discharged. Or you may return to visit and follow up with the patient as the medical intervention continues. If no new concerns present themselves, you may not need to do more than this at each subsequent visit.

Spiritual Assessment Worksheet

In addition to the previous recommendations, you may want to develop your own assessment sheet to organize your questions and compile pertinent information for later review. I would suggest the following approach developed by this author.

Belief – What is your **belief** system? Are you a person of faith and if so, what is it that you believe? What is it that gives your life meaning and purpose? How active are you in pursuing your faith?

Support – What type of personal support system do you have? Is your family close and available to assist you? What about your community, friends, church? Are they supportive?

Cope – How do you feel you are dealing with your stay here? What about the diagnosis? Do you have questions or concerns? What about your family, are they having any problems with your diagnosis?

Next Steps – What other problems or concerns might you have? Is there anything that I or the medical staff can assist you with during your stay here?[29]

Depending upon the outcome of the questions above, you may decide you need to follow through with a more extensive evaluation. Patient history, family history, spiritual history are all key elements of a thorough evaluation of the patient's condition. Along with this, you may want to evaluate where the patient is now on their faith journey, and where they would like to go.

---

[29] This worksheet is available in the back of your book.

If you think about it, this is much the same as the system a medical doctor uses. I recently switched doctors as my family practitioner had retired. When I went to the office to meet this doctor for the first time, he wanted to know all about my medical history, my family history, and any problems I was currently experiencing. To this basic history and data collection, the doctor reviewed all the diagnostic tests and procedures that I had obtained.

After determining his final diagnoses, he discussed his results with me and suggested a plan for my care; this included appropriate interventions. It was then up to me to follow his suggestions or decline. It was and is my right to make the final determination. I can accept his plan of care in part, in full, or look for a new doctor if I prefer. Those are my rights as a patient. Your patient has those same rights.

The only time you have a legal right, and even a legal obligation to go against the patient's wishes is in the case of imminent danger. Imminent danger may include: abuse, suicide, or mental incompetence. When in doubt, report your concerns to your superior immediately to determine your moral and legal obligations as a clinician.

We have covered both basic and thorough spiritual assessments. Once you have all your data collected, what next? Next you need to prayerfully analyze all the information and determine your diagnoses. What problems do you feel need to be addressed and what interventions would you like to propose?

What that intervention looks like will be determined by the problem, the patient, and the time and resources that you and the patient have available. Once you have the full spiritual assessment, determined your diagnoses, and finalized the interventions, you will be ready to create a spiritual care plan.

So, where does the seminary student, lay leader, chaplain begin this process? Let us begin by looking at the following case study.

Case Study

Jenny (not her real name), was admitted to the hospital in acute respiratory distress. Weeks prior to her admission she had been diagnosed with bronchitis and the doctor prescribed antibiotics and an inhaler. Weeks went by and she returned to the doctor several times, presenting with shortness of breath and growing weakness. The doctor listened to her lungs but could find no reason for her continued complaints. Soon he became impatient with her return visits, so he sent her home and told her to rest.

Her condition continued to worsen and she could no longer sleep in her bed but had to sleep sitting up straight; her appetite waned. Finally, in acute respiratory distress, her husband drove her back to the doctor. His auscultation of her lungs remained the same, nothing wrong, he begrudgingly sent her to the hospital. Upon admission, an x-ray proved that she had severe pneumonia in both lungs. Intravenous fluids, medications, and oxygen were finally prescribed.

Three days later, Jenny's condition continued to deteriorate. She ate little but gained 20 lbs. of fluid during her first three days in the hospital. Unable to tolerate the IV fluids, her heart had become enlarged. Sleep was the one thing she needed the most; but sleep was elusive. Jenny feared that if she fell asleep she would die.

The nurses were kind and understanding but did not know how to help. If only a chaplain had been available. A chaplain's assessment may have revealed the underlying reason Jenny was so fearful; her own sister had died of pneumonia in her sleep.

As demonstrated by this true story, the need for chaplains is real and their role dynamic. Medical staff are not always equipped to care for the spiritual needs of their patients. How might the availability of a pastoral caregiver have changed the dynamics of this story, had someone been there to not only listen and pray, but to assess, diagnose, and treat? Let us dig deeper into the story.

For months preceding the hospital admission, Jenny had been experiencing dreams. They were dreams about the death of her sister. The memories of the dreams would carry through with her into her waking hours, and tears would sometimes flow unexpectedly. A full family history, and spiritual assessment may have been enlightening and helpful. Let us take the dreams to start with.

The dreams were about the bitter cold morning in February when her sister was found in her crib not breathing. Jenny remembered the details vividly even though she had only been four years old at the time. She remembers her father scrapping the windows of his car as he got ready to go to work. Her sister had not awakened yet, so Jenny's mother went to check on her.

That is when Jenny was urgently summoned to get her father as the baby of four months was not breathing. Activity happened quickly after that, the doctor, family, and others came to the house. Jenny did not understand what was happening but she knew that it was bad. She hid under the bed.

Little of significance was remembered after that. No memory of funeral plans or service. Not even a memory of discussion about where the sister had gone… she was just gone. I suspect Jenny was shielded from the cold truth. So, years later, she began to have dreams about the death. Those dreams began the process of grieving some 40 years later.

Then she got pneumonia herself, and the fear of dying like her sister had in her sleep, became a viable threat. Jenny had some issues regarding grief and dying that were causing a significant impact on her health. Added to the physical problems the infection had caused, it was worsened by her fear of falling asleep and not waking up. We know that uncovering this underlying problem and helping Jenny confront her fears could have a significant impact on her recovery.

Creating a Spiritual Care Plan

What is an accepted standard for creating a spiritual care plan? In the document, Standards of Practice for Chaplains in Acute Care Settings, The Association of Professional Chaplains in Standard 2 of Section 1 lists this:

"An assessment and determination of a plan of care that contributes to the overall care of the patient that is measurable and documented."[30]

I believe this standard should apply to anyone functioning in the capacity of a healthcare chaplain, not just in acute care settings. The standard for professional spiritual care is to provide both an assessment and a plan of care. The plan of care needs to be both measurable and documented. It needs to be professionally done and equal in quality to the care plans of other members of the medical care team. This would include the care plans of nurses, social workers, and others.

How Can the Medical Staff Participate in the Spiritual Care Plan?

It is important to differentiate which interventions are strictly delivered by the chaplain, and what is to be a part of the overall care plan with other staff participating. While the chaplain over-sees all spiritual care, and develops the care plan for spiritual care, certain interventions can be reinforced by the whole team. The chaplain is responsible for overseeing and training the rest of the staff regarding spiritual care interventions as is appropriate to carry out the activities on the care plan for which they will assist.

Remember your care plan will be subject to the rules and regulations of the institution where you are performing your duties. You are responsible for knowing and following the guidelines and making sure your care plan does so as well.

---

[30] http://www.professionalchaplains.org/files/professional_standards/standards_of_practice/standards_practice_professional_chaplains_acute_care.pdf

Where Do We Start?

There is no greater source of wisdom and direction than the guidance Holy Spirit can provide. Prayerfully proceed with what you know to do, and anticipate the Lord's guidance. Be open to the leading of the Spirit, praying for discernment and godly wisdom.

Then, begin by completing the full spiritual assessment and family history. Once you have all the data collected, you will want to list each problem you identified in your assessment. Name each concern on your list; such as poor self-image, fear of dying, unforgiveness, bitterness, lack of support system, marital difficulties, end of life concerns, etc. Anything your data collection can support as a diagnosis, list on your spiritual care plan. These are your diagnoses.

In the case study of Jenny, two of the primary diagnoses could be unresolved grief and fear of death. Even though she did not die of her pneumonia, the threat in her mind was real and tangible. It affected her ability to fall asleep and hindered the healing process. An in-depth history and assessment may have uncovered other concerns as well.

Create a full list and then begin to prioritize the diagnoses in order from the most crucial to the least. How do you know which one to address first? Some may find it helpful to list the needs in the order shown by Maslow's hierarchy of needs. The most crucial needs would be on the bottom, and then work your way up. [31]

---

[31] Image is public domain. https://commons.wikimedia.org/wiki/File:Maslow_hierarchy_of_needs.jpg

Self-actualizing needs — Self-aware personal growth

Esteem needs — Self-worth, accomplishment

Social needs — Belonging, love, family

Security — Safety, steady job, insurance

Physiological — Food, water, shelter, air, warmth

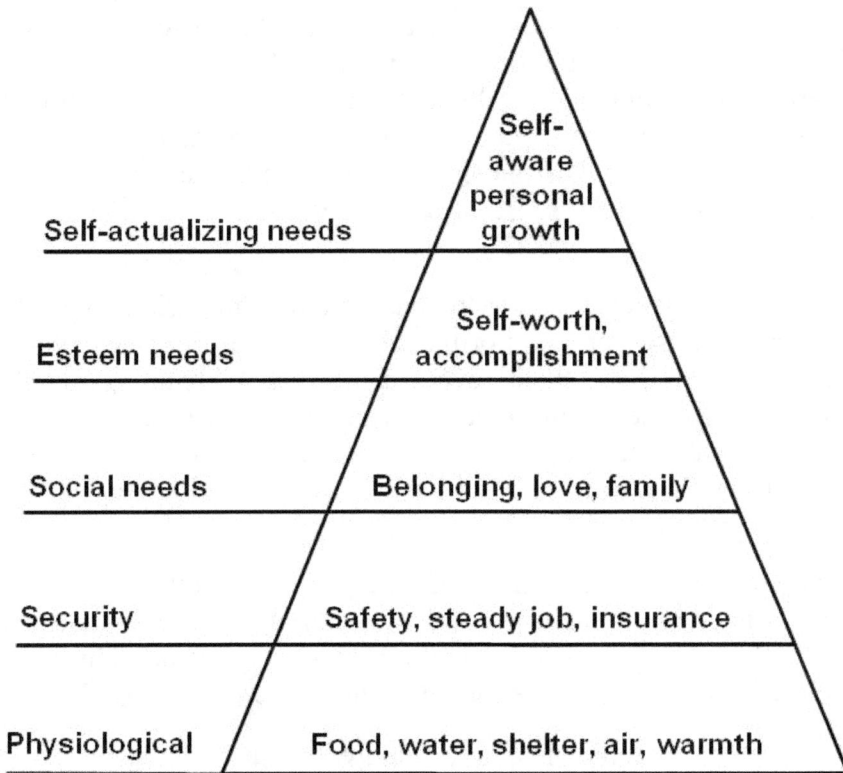

Maslow's hierarchy of needs (1943)

Remember your care plan must be clear and concise so that the whole medical team understands. What part of the plan the team will assist with and what part is to be exclusively fulfilled by the chaplain should be evident. The diagnosis, goals, and interventions need to be specific and measurable.

The diagnosis listed on the plan should clearly state when the problem began, if it is directly related to the health problem, what may be causing the problem, and how this problem may affect the patient's medical care overall. The specific goals for each diagnosis must be outlined before any interventions can be determined.

What are some specific goals that we may choose for our patient, Jenny? First, the most basic of needs as displayed on the Maslow's chart at the bottom is physiological. The patient is having difficulty breathing and is concerned she may cease to breathe in her sleep and die. The spiritual diagnosis is fear of dying. The goal is to raise the patient's comfort/ sense of safety level so she can sleep. The intervention?

Alerting the medical team to the patient's fear may trigger an order for heart and oxygen monitoring. This may be the reassurance she needs that in the unlikely event she stopped breathing, an immediate response by the medical team would prevent her dying. Her spiritual need may qualify her for this medical intervention even if the team does not feel her medical condition warrants the use of monitoring.

An additional intervention that the chaplain may outline in the care plan is to reinforce as often as is appropriate and reasonable that her full recovery is expected, providing that is true. This is an intervention that the whole medical team can work on together.

- The problem is fear associated with fear of dying.

- The goal is to raise the patient's comfort level and increase her sense of safety measurable by increased time of relaxed sleep.

- One possible intervention is increased communication with the patient regarding her anticipated outcome. Other interventions may include prayer, frequent monitoring and reassurance by staff, relaxing music at bedtime, etc.

- The results of the intervention are measurable. Documentation of improved sleep patterns, changes in patient's mood and outlook may all support a successful intervention.

Let us review the primary concepts set forth in this important chapter. Much of the work of the chaplain will be determined first by a preliminary assessment. If a need to work with the patient for one or more additional visits exists, the next step is to move forward with a more thorough history and spiritual assessment.

Following the gathering of all data, the chaplain will evaluate the information and create a list of diagnoses. These diagnoses will be listed in order of importance and appropriate goals established. Finally, appropriate interventions will be created and documented in the care plan.

The care plan must be documented in a clear and concise manner and become a part of the overall patient plan of care. Cooperation of the patient and appropriate staff members will require good communication and documentation skills by the chaplain.

Remember, you are a part of a team of professionals and co-operation and mutual respect for the part each play in the overall care of the patient is essential for optimal patient care.

No longer is the chaplain limited to merely listening, praying, and reading of scripture. There is an opportunity for and an expectation of professional caregiving on the spiritual level by chaplains in this era. Medical practitioners, Medicare, and (JCAHO) the accrediting commission for hospitals, have all acknowledged the need for whole patient care and that spiritual care is essential for optimal patient outcomes.

Relationship is the Key

As we bring this important chapter to a close, I want to emphasize the importance of relationship in all that we do.

First, our relationship with the Lord, if not saved by his grace I would have no reason to write this book. We cannot minister to others from an empty well. We must have experienced salvation and been filled by his love and spirit to have anything in our own vessel to share with others.

Second, comes our relationship with others. In the standards of practice discussed earlier in this chapter, the preamble reads like this:

"Chaplaincy care is grounded in initiating, developing and deepening, and bringing to an appropriate close, a mutual and empathic relationship with the patient, family, and/ or staff. The development of a genuine relationship is at the core of chaplaincy care and underpins, even enables, all the other dimensions of chaplaincy care to occur. It is assumed that all of the standards are addressed within the context of such relationships."[32]

One might say it is a fulfillment of the two greatest laws as set forth by Jesus in Matthew 22:37-39

"You shall love the Lord your God with all your heart, with all your soul, and with all your mind. This is the greatest and foremost commandment. The second is like it, You shall love your neighbor as yourself."

AMEN!

---

[32] http://www.professionalchaplains.org/files/professional_standards/standards_of_practice/standards_practice_professional_chaplains_acute_care.pdf

Chapter Four Questions

1. What was Paul Pruyser's contribution to the evolution of the chaplain's role?

2. Who introduced the term 7 x 7 and what does it have to do with spiritual assessment?

3. What is the purpose of a spiritual care plan?

4. How do you determine which problem to address first when more than one needs your attention?

Chapter Five: Diagnosis Based Considerations

While a chaplain may choose to contribute to the welfare of patients in many different settings, some specialize in one specific area. For instance, one may work for hospice or palliative care, others choose pediatrics or obstetrics. Some prefer the emotionally charged and rapidly evolving environment of the ER. One is not better than another, simply different.

Choosing a specialty does not mean you are incapable of helping all patients, it simply means you have developed a knowledge base and skill set for one specific area. You may have life experience or personal medical expertise that helps you relate more closely to others in the same situation. We tend to minister out of the comfort that we once experienced for ourselves. It becomes personal. The fact that we can empathize with the patient does not release us from the responsibility to remain objective.

Each of the specialty areas has specific diagnosis based considerations. As we highlight some of the differences from one medical expertise to another, it is not meant to be a full exposé on any one topic. Should you choose to specialize in one of the following areas, you will want to do an in-depth study in the area that you have chosen.

Palliative Care

"Both palliative care and hospice care provide comfort. But palliative care can begin at diagnosis, and at the same time as treatment.

Hospice care begins after treatment of the disease is stopped and when it is clear that the person is not going to survive the illness.

Hospice care is usually offered only when the person is expected to live 6 months or less."[33]

Chaplains who work with patients in palliative or hospice care have a unique set of circumstances and symptoms that they must address. This includes in part, problems with chronic pain, discomfort, sleeplessness, loss of appetite, loss of independence, and depression. Questions regarding life purpose and potential end of life concerns; many ask where is God and why me? Doesn't God care? Patients and their families need a spiritual caregiver to come alongside and walk with them during this time of difficulty.

As stated above, palliative care may begin from the point of diagnosis. The patient is not necessarily facing imminent death, but rather prolonged life changing health concerns. Many times, self-esteem, self-image, and life purpose is affected and an acceptance of this new life normal comes slowly. Chaplains help patients and families transition through this difficult time.

The normal stages of grief and loss must be traversed before acceptance can be realized, acceptance of this new reality. The chaplain guides them on the journey. We know when traveling somewhere new, a guide can be invaluable. Travel guides know how to avoid known pitfalls, side step land mines, and insure safe arrival to the destination. The journey is easier with a guide.

As guide, the chaplain meets the patient where he or she is on their faith journey respecting and supporting their personal belief system and culture. It is the chaplain's responsibility to help the patient utilize their own personal faith and beliefs as spiritual coping tools, regardless of the chaplain's personal faith affiliations.

Along with assisting them engage their personal faith as a source of peace and strength, the chaplain also acts as an ambassador, bridging the gap of understanding in the medical environment.

[33] https://medlineplus.gov/ency/patientinstructions/000536.htm

Patients may or may not have a comfort level with the terms and procedures confronting them in the medical facility.

For some, the change in their normal routine may have been abrupt. One day they were working, raising their family, and participating in social functions; then suddenly an illness, disease, or accident occurred disrupting their life. Some may liken this to having the rug pulled out from under them. Getting their bearings to this new reality may take time and adjustment. The chaplain is there to help them understand this new reality and help them comprehend how to adjust.

I can relate on a personal level to how difficult it is for patients and their families. In my role as a pastoral care giver, I am often called upon to accompany the family into consultations with doctors. I can comfort the family as their advocate, but also have the needed medical knowledge to comprehend what the doctors and nurses are communicating. Long after the doctor has left the room, the family often has questions about the meaning of what the doctor meant and the possible consequences. My knowledge of medical terms, protocol, and practices is helpful to those I am there to support. Again, it is the chaplain's responsibility to bridge the gap within the scope of their own knowledge and capabilities.

Patients who benefit from palliative care are patients with cancer, cardiac related issues, neurological concerns such as stroke, patients dealing with complex surgical procedures and repeat hospitalizations. Any serious illness that has an impact on quality or length of life would potentially benefit from palliative care involvement. The chaplain is a significant member of such a team. The goal of palliative care is to improve symptom management, quality of life, and in some cases, improve the chance of survival.

Hospice

While palliative care begins from the point of diagnosis and can be associated with chronic disease, hospice care only begins when treatment stops and the end of life is anticipated within six months.

Hospice chaplaincy focuses on comfort measures and processing through the end of life concerns. Many emotions such as anger, depression, and regret can take root; it is the responsibility of the chaplain to help the patient transition through to acceptance and peace.

This job description posted on Study.com states that "hospice chaplains provide spiritual support to terminally ill patients and their families." It further defines their role as a member of the interdisciplinary team with responsibility for spiritual assessments of the patient which is to include the mental, emotional, physical, and spiritual stresses. As is customary for chaplains practicing in most other areas of allied health, they create and carryout an individualized plan of care.

Duties that a hospice chaplain may be expected to perform are providing communion, bereavement/memorial services, when the patient dies, as well as phone calls and visits to the deceased patient's family. The chaplain is not there to replace the patient's clergy (if they are also involved), but rather to provide support and assistance as needed. When a chaplain is available, there is no reason for a patient to die alone.

Ultimately, the chaplain is an instrument of peace in the dilemma facing families when a loved one is dying. First, the chaplain helps the patient come into acceptance of the impending death and finding spiritual and emotional peace. Secondly, they help the whole family process through the stages of grief. Some need help in saying goodbye.

Because emotions often intensify during this time, conflict resolutions skills are key to maintaining a peaceful environment. The family's interactions with one another and with the patient can become tense, but ideally, they will work through this time to reach reconciliation, forgiveness, and finally acceptance and peace.

For more information on helping families process through grief, refer to the book, *Grief Relief*, by Dr. Stan DeKoven. [34]

For a list of standards of practice for chaplains in palliative and hospice care, please go to the website of Professional Chaplains.org.[35]

Acute Care Chaplaincy

Some chaplains specialize in acute care. This may include coronary care, intensive care, open heart, and stepdown units, etc. By the very nature of such units, it can become intense and traumatic for the patient, the family, and the staff. Circumstances are often tenuous and can become critical in a matter of moments. This can be stressful for all involved.

The patient may or may not be conscious and aware of their condition. It is therefore the family in need of support and guidance when the crisis calls for life changing decisions.

Some may be guided by a living will, or have medical power of attorney to act on the patient's behalf. In these cases, the patient's desire for end of life medical care is outlined in the will. The authority to act on behalf of the patient is often given in advance should the patient be unable to communicate their wishes for themselves.

In the living will, one can designate their wishes regarding the use of a ventilator, CPR, IV fluids and nutrition, administration of certain drugs, diagnostic tests, dialysis, transfusion, surgery, even food and water in the event the patient has a serious illness or becomes permanently comatose.

---

[34] DeKoven, Stan E. Ph. D, author Grief Relief, Vision Publishing of Ramona, Ca; March 2004; www.booksbyvision.org

[35] http://www.professionalchaplains.org/files/professional_standards/standards_of_practice/standards_of_practice_hospice_palliative_care.pdf

Some choose palliative care only for a dying patient. This usually means no life prolonging interventions but comfort measures only. When no life prolonging interventions are wanted, a "do not resuscitate" order may be initiated. In the event death occurs, the medical staff knows not to resuscitate or perform CPR.

All such situations can leave the family in need of guidance and support. Therefore, the family is frequently the recipient of the chaplain's care in such units. Sitting with the family, praying with them, consoling them as a loved one's life hangs in the balance are all important in such cases. Families faced with the decision of when to pull the plug on the ventilator, go through a whole host of emotions. Chaplains can be instrumental in helping them come to terms with the loss of the loved one.

Emergency Room/Crisis Intervention

Chaplains assigned to the emergency department must be ready to act on a moment's notice. Chaplain Lewis, (not his real name) remembered the following case. He was in the emergency room talking with the social worker when the first victims of a multiple car accident arrived.

The mother was driving her two young daughters when a drunk driver struck their van. The team did all that they could but the mother died from her injuries. The staff was in the process of notifying next of kin.

In the meantime, the second patient who had arrived at the same time was one of her daughters. The team was working to care for her injuries when she became aware that her mother had not made it. She became hysterical before other family members could arrive. The chaplain stepped in to console the young girl while the team worked on her medical needs.

The chaplain, nor any of the other staff know what tragedy or triumph they may face in any given day. Crisis intervention is a daily occurrence. Staff must be ready and willing to respond.

Many other types of crises await a chaplain willing to take an assignment in the emergency room. Victims of rape, abuse, physical assault, domestic violence first present for treatment in the emergency room.

As a nurse, I never wanted to work in the ER. In fact, those who enjoyed working in that type of environment tended to be the type who thrived on the excitement. It takes a very special person to work on a continuing basis in the emergency department.

One never knows when one will walk in with a knife buried in the chest, a missing limb, or some other horrific circumstances. Crises intervention tools and conflict management skills are imperative for anyone wishing to assist in this specialty area.

Renal Dialysis

Patients who find themselves with the need of renal dialysis are confronting a permanent, chronic condition that will alter their lifestyle and ability to care for a family or hold a job. Accommodations must be made for the life sustaining treatments. The only hope a patient with permanent kidney failure and dialysis has for improvement is a potential kidney transplant. Rejection of the kidney and need for medication to prevent rejection are still concerns for the patient fortunate enough to obtain a viable organ.

Patients who require dialysis have several options, but any option they choose is time consuming and life altering. Patients who opt to have their dialysis in a center must commit to a minimum of 3 visits per week and each visit is usually between three and five hours. Even the patients who choose peritoneal dialysis at home, still find their lifestyle drastically altered to accommodate the lifesaving dialysis treatments.

Their dietary habits and blood work must be closely monitored to prevent crises. This permanent condition forces the patient and family to adjust their lifestyle dramatically. As with any change of this magnitude, the patient must be encouraged and supported to maintain a sense of hope and self-worth. Patients and their families are exceptionally vulnerable to emotional conflict relating to their disease process and to the potential of altered family responsibilities and expectations.

I remember one young mother who suffered with kidney failure. Her small children required her care, so another caregiver was necessary to provide the needed care while mom sat for her treatments three times a week. In addition, this became a huge financial burden on the family as she was unable to work.

When the family wanted to go away on vacation, it required a tremendous amount of planning. She could not go unless she located a facility that would do her treatments at the destination where she wanted to vacation. Not only was her freedom and independence compromised, it also affected her husband and small children.

The chaplain in these cases may be responsible not only for providing spiritual support, but also counseling and conflict management. Adjusting to an altered self-image and lack of independence can be difficult, especially for younger patients.

In addition, the blood pressure of patients receiving dialysis may crash very suddenly during the treatment. Although staff monitor the vitals of the patient continuously, the threat of a sudden drop is very real and can be frightening for the patient. Staff do their best to prevent this from occurring, nevertheless it does happen occasionally. Continuous support and reassurance is needed.

Pediatric/Obstetrics

Chaplains in the obstetrics department have a difficult task. While the birth of a healthy baby is the goal of everyone, that is not always the outcome. Families trying to prevent a miscarriage or premature birth may also appear in the obstetrics unit for help. The crisis is real, and the pain profound for any family who has struggled to become pregnant and deliver a healthy baby. The loss of a baby at any stage of development is heartbreaking.

The risk to mother and baby even at full term can be tremendous. Any number of problems can develop to put both mother and child at risk. While complications can be minimized by good obstetrical care, not everything is preventable. A sudden rise in the blood pressure of the mother, an umbilical cord that becomes wrapped about the infant's neck as it descends into the birth canal, a placenta that detaches from the wall of the uterus prematurely can all place the mother and child at risk.

While the obstetrics unit is a place of anticipated celebration of new life, death at times is also present; the mother who hemorrhages or suffers stroke, or the infant that is stillborn. Unfortunately, we deal with tragedies alongside of the many triumphs. The chaplain must be ready for anything and prepared to offer hope even in the direst of circumstances.

The pediatrics unit offers its own challenges. Families may be split apart by illness or injury of one of their little ones. Sudden catastrophic illnesses can take a great toll on all family members.

One of my own grandchildren was diagnosed with a golf ball sized tumor on the brain. Just one week earlier this happy little seven-year-old showed no signs of illness. Then suddenly, there was a migraine headache accompanied by nausea and vomiting. For three days, we assumed she had a virus. On the third day she saw her pediatrician, a very astute pediatrician who suspected something more was going on and ordered an emergency MRI. A few hours later the diagnosis was in and she was on her way to children's hospital.

We experienced shock, how could this happen to our little girl? I was the director of pastoral care, the one who helped others in times of crisis. Now I needed the same care that I had so often offered to others. No one is immune.

This story does have a good outcome. The tumor was 90% removed and almost ten years later, the remaining portion is without change. We are so grateful to our God for his mercy. Not all cases progress as well.

The need for spiritual care for all age groups is obvious. No matter who you are, someday you may need someone to come alongside and hold you up when you think you can no longer go on.

In my case, a spiritual caregiver was present with my whole family for two full days at the hospital. I was so distraught, I could not even pray for myself. This couple, the senior pastors at the church where I ministered, prayed with us, comforted us, and gave us hope. I am so grateful for the assistance and peace they brought into our crisis.

Psychiatry and Substance Abuse

"The doctor is effective only when he himself is affected. Only the wounded physician heals." Carl Jung [36]

This is an interesting quote used by a Seattle based chaplain's group to explain the premise upon which their outreach to the homeless has been founded. They assert that most of them have been touched in some way by the pain of mental illness and or substance abuse and therefore as "wounded healers" they reach out to heal others. They have been doing so for some thirty years now.

While you may or may not agree with the premise presented in the Carl Jung quote, I can tell you that each of us has the compassion and love of Christ from which we can empathize. We all have a wealth of hope from which to console and encourage others that struggle in these two areas; regardless whether we have been personally afflicted.

---

[36] http://www.azquotes.com/quote/1200463

I have been ministering in a home for women recovering from addiction for some three years now. My connection with them and their circumstances is real. Have I ever suffered from drug or alcohol abuse? Emphatically, no! I have never tried illicit drugs and have never been addicted to alcohol. My own grandfather was an alcoholic and I knew that steady consumption of this substance was something I wanted to avoid.

Although I have never personally experienced drug addiction or suffered from alcoholism, I have found a connection card that makes me effective just the same. I understand the pain of abuse. Abuse in any form, self-inflicted or as the victim of another's abuse is still abuse. I know this pain on a personal level. I encourage others by sharing my story, my journey to freedom. I am no longer the victim of abuse. I share my tragedies and triumphs, and they connect with me there as one who knows abuse, and as one who has overcome. My testimony gives them hope. So perhaps the wounded warrior does apply, at least in this case. I minister to others out of the comfort I have received.

Even if you have not been affected by either of these two problems, you can still connect with these patients and offer the healing of God. You bring the very presence of God into the room with you, and he is the greatest healer of them all. Therefore, as Chaplains, you have the help of God's presence to offer to those in need.

These specific areas of healthcare are often based upon abnormalities that are more mental and emotionally based rather than physical. Although some physical maladies may be contributing factors, those affected by mental illness and substance abuse benefit greatly from counseling, rehab programs, and twelve step programs.

When these patients first present to the medical facility or rehab home for treatment, it is usually because they are in crisis. During this critical time, the primary goal should be comfort and listening.

Helping the patient find peace in which to heal should be your first objective.

You may be able to read healing scriptures and pray. Each situation is different and you will need to use your own spiritual discernment to lead you in such matters. After the crisis has been averted more long-term interventions can be initiated.

The very nature of the highly successful twelve step program relies on a spiritual component for recovery. The ministry of a chaplain in both areas of healthcare will be greatly beneficial to all involved.

Home Health

We have just two more areas of healthcare to highlight in this section. The first one is Home Health. Patients who are served by home health agencies suffer from one or more diagnoses that keep them homebound. Often isolated and lonely, these patients need a companion and spiritual guide just as much as those in a facility. For many, the healthcare team may be the only regular visits they get.

Chaplains can be very beneficial in aiding the staff and the patient during this time. The patient's prognosis and personal needs will determine the spiritual care plan you develop. The problem may be temporary and full health anticipated, or it may be the beginning of the "end of life" journey. Either way, you as a chaplain can play a key role in guiding the patient along the journey.

Disabilities

Finally, we want to talk for just a moment about the needs of those with disabilities. What is a disability exactly? Usually it is defined as an inability to do what others normally do. It is something that limits the person's movements, senses, or activities. Another term often used is, handicapped.

Let us give some thought to that definition however. By nature, it defines another's normal as abnormal, somehow inferring that they do not measure up. What if, however, we were to reframe our terminology? Empowering the person rather than disabling them?

This is a concept explored by author *Gunnar A. Cerda, BCC,* Manager of Pastoral Care for Ohio Health Grady Memorial Hospital in Delaware, Ohio. He writes:

> *"When empowering language is used about persons with disabilities, the metaphors can shift the focus from a person's limitations, to a perspective of ability, and from patient or diagnosis to personhood. Re-imagining the language we use in our professional practice can provide improved pathways of empathy, understanding, and communication."*[37]

Chaplain Cerda would have good reason to know since his own son was diagnosed with Asperger Syndrome, which is a form of autism. Despite the world's prognosis of limitations, with the proper tools and support, his son excels in his areas of giftedness which exceeds the common norms of others who do not profess disability. Although special accommodations are made for his son's limitations, that is not to say that he suffers. Rather, because accommodations are made he excels over others in certain areas.

We sometimes use words such as "suffering from" when referring to someone who has a handicap. Gunnar A. Cerda writes:

> *"Not all persons with disabilities describe themselves as suffering; many would describe their lives as happy and productive. Not to mention that suffering implies spiritual or emotional distress, which all persons will encounter through-out life and through many situations unrelated to ability."*

Perhaps one man's disability is another man's gift. It is certainly a matter of perspective. Those with perceived disabilities in one area may excel far above the norm in other areas. The words we use,

---

[37] https://csupalliativecare.org/disability/

the terminology we frame our responses with, can create a limiting or an empowering environment. We get to choose how we wish to influence our patients with our words.

Chapter Five Questions

1. What special considerations are unique to patients and their families in the Acute Care Units?

2. Patients in hospice require assistance with end of life decisions. How would you address the needs of these patients?

3. Which specialty area would you be most attracted to and why?

4. The writer addressed people with special needs and disabilities. What point stood out the most when you read this section?

Chapter Six: The Future of Hospital Chaplaincy

"The hospital is a place of paradox, of contradictions and blurred realities. A place where many of our patients' fondest hopes and prayers are miraculously answered. A place where many of their deepest fears and agonies are painfully endured. It is the place where hospital chaplains do ministry."

Lawrence E. Holst - Hospital Ministry: The Role of the Chaplain Today[38]

As we look forward to the future of healthcare chaplaincy, perhaps it would be wise to revisit where we have been. While chaplaincy can be traced back to biblical roots, healthcare chaplaincy has existed only since medical facilities have been in existence. We know that patients were cared for in the homes of family members. Even near the turn of the 19th century hospitals (first known as alms houses) were only for the poor who had no one to care for them.

Hospitals were established first by the church, and the church's clergy cared for the spiritual needs of the sick. As the footprint of hospitals grew larger and the demand for care escalated, it quickly became a profitable business enterprise. As leadership of the major hospitals became more secularized, the need for chaplains became apparent. Who would care for the spiritual needs of the sick in a secular environment? However, the role and authority of the chaplain had very humble beginnings.

The chaplain did not have the power and authority to occupy a seat on the patient's interdisciplinary team immediately. That was a role that evolved over time as the "authorities" within the medical

---

[38] Holst, Lawrence E.; editor, Hospital Ministry, The role of the Chaplain Today, ISBN 1-59752-814-5 by Wipf and Stock Publishers, in 2006, Eugene, Oregon.

community began to take note and respected the contribution a chaplain had to offer. Even Medicare and JCAHO recognized the value chaplains provided in the growing trend toward whole patient care.

With this recognition also came the demand for the establishment of professional standards of care and training. If the chaplains were to be paid by hospital/Medicare dollars, then the standards by which their work was executed must be measurably of a quality that entitled them to the respect of a medical care clinician. That standard could not be based solely upon the endorsement of the church.

The interdisciplinary team is a team of professionals, and to include chaplains on this team required professionalism in the expertise they practiced. For this reason, the need for training, education, and certification became necessary. This certification made chaplains accountable not only to the medical facility that employed them, but also to the educators on boards of certification in their field of chaplaincy. Quality and accountability are important, even in ministry.

Let us fast forward.

Even as the role of chaplains has evolved, so has the role of hospitals and other medical facilities that provide patient care. While hospitalizations for routine medical problems became customary in the 1900's, the pendulum has since swung in the opposite direction. As the secularization of hospitals took root and the funding was established through medical insurance and public assistance, the need to downsize the number of days a patient stayed in the hospital began. Why might you ask? For the most part, it was in the interest of saving money.

The demand to do more in less time has caused the practice of medicine to change abruptly. Surgeries that would have kept the patient hospitalized for days or perhaps even weeks, have now become more routine and are often accomplished in same day surgery units.

This trend is not necessarily bad. It benefits the patient as well; the longer a patient stays in the hospital the more apt they are to develop a hospital based infection. Often, if care can be provided safely at home, the patient is more comfortable and happy. There they can be surrounded by friends and family, not the starkness of the hospital environment.

Isn't it amazing how some things appear to come full circle? Just as it was in the early 1900's with patients being cared for in their homes by family, so we see a return to home based care. However, the quality of medical care in the home has evolved as well. Families can care for the patient with the assistance of a professional home care team.

Patients that are homebound can still receive the professional care of doctors, nurses, physical therapists, nursing assistants, even social workers, and chaplains. Whole patient care has evolved into a home-based business and the patient benefits by being able to stay where they are most comfortable.

No longer does a patient need to go to the hospital to get vital IV antibiotics, a home health nurse provides that care in the comfort of their own home. They no longer need to go to a rehab unit for physical and occupational therapy, that is available at home as well, and performed by trained professionals.

While the location where medical services are performed has changed, the need for care has not changed. There are still patients in need of care, and that includes chaplain's services. So how does this trend in medical services affect the care given by the chaplain? I'm so glad you asked!

In 2012 the Rev. Dr. Walter J. Smith, president and CEO of HealthCare Chaplaincy stated this:

"The current system in professional chaplaincy is not sustainable and we must develop and embrace a different mode. Without an empirical base that validates the outcomes of their professional work, chaplaincy as a profession will remain on the margin of health care, and not be able to justify further investment of limited health care dollars to support its professional endeavors."[39]

Professional standards and practice are mandatory if chaplaincy is to remain a viable and fundable endeavor[40].

Chaplains must go where the patient goes; to rehab units, to renal dialysis units, to nursing homes, same day surgery units, and yes into the homes of homebound patients. Even within the confines of the hospital, chaplains must alter the way they provide care to their patient because of reduced stays.

They may need to hang out in the ER, in waiting rooms, or meet with families in the hall. Let us remember, the need for care is still there, it is just the location where those services are performed that may have changed. The tapestry healthcare is painted on is ever changing, but the need for healthcare and spiritual care has not. The role of the chaplain must change to remain relevant in the changing environment where health care is received.

While it is impossible to accurately predict the future, the trends lead us to a path that will keep us abreast of each new change. If each of us is willing to be flexible and adaptable as changes come, the role of chaplains will remain. Where does a minister go to meet the needs of God's people? The answer is easy, wherever God's people go, and to wherever God has called. If God's people are there, they have spiritual needs that you can provide for.

---

[39]   https://www.healthcarechaplaincy.org/news-events/entry/gaps-in-profession-still-ring-true.html

[40]   As previously stated, most chaplains are either part-time, volunteer, or self-funded. For more information or for coaching on how to raise funds to support your ministry please contact ksmith@vision.edu

One new wave of the future which is already being utilized is chaplains via online chat. Following on the wave of the future in telemedicine. Healthcare chaplains can extend their reach using social media and the internet.

They may listen and respond to such questions as, "why am I in pain," or "am I being punished"? Skype, Facetime, and online chat rooms are just a few of the possible options for this new mode of communication.

The service, "Chat with a Chaplain" was launched in 2015 out of a New York based non-profit organization. One can now dial up a chaplain and ask those hard-hitting questions. One can only guess where all these new technologies will lead. Be assured, where there is a need, the chaplain will be there to bridge the gap and fill it.

Another recent development in providing chaplain services is HCCN TV, the spiritual care network. They have developed inter-active telehealth programs. Two of their programs are Spiritual Care Connect and Palliative Connect.

The role of the chaplain continues to evolve alongside the changes in healthcare delivery systems. Advancements and changes in the way care is delivered raises new ethical questions for the healthcare team. When those questions arise, the chaplain is a welcome voice adding value and biblical guidance helping the whole interdisciplinary team approach the topics and resolve their concerns. Thus indeed, the chaplain is an integral and valued member of the interdisciplinary team.

What role will chaplains play in healthcare in the future? Let us listen as one chaplain shares a story of healing for her patient, Mary (not her real name).

The chaplain begins by explaining that her patient had recently had heart surgery and was on a ventilator, therefore she could not talk. However, Mary would often reach out to staff when any came near. Her nurse described her as "needy". The chaplain approached her bedside and sat down.

Once again, Mary reached out to touch her hand with tears in her eyes. The woman's pain was more than physical. That was obvious. Since she was unable to talk, it was difficult to know what the problem could be. That is when the chaplain noticed the bible at her bedside. Obviously, Mary was a woman of faith.

She offered to pray for her and Mary squeezed her hand as if to say yes. After praying for healing and peace, the chaplain read some healing scriptures from Psalms. The next day Mary's sister arrived to visit and the chaplain introduced herself.

That is when she learned that Mary had lost her husband of 60 years just a few days before she entered the hospital. No wonder Mary was so distraught, she was grieving and could not adequately express the pain she was experiencing. After that, the chaplain visited Mary's bedside as frequently as possible.

She offered to play soothing music, pray for her, read scriptures, and just be there to hold her hand. She even did her best to bring up Mary's husband, and give voice to what she thought Mary may be feeling. Mary seemed relieved to hear someone address her pain, and the tears flowed freely. Over the next few weeks, Mary's condition continued to improve, and her emotions began to stabilize.

Chaplains can and do make a difference in people's lives. They heal with their words, their touch, and their caring. Did God call you to the ministry of caregiving? Did he call you to fulfill the role of a chaplain? If your answer to those questions is yes, then your future is secure in the chaplain ministry. If you remain humble, flexible, adaptable, accountable, and willing... there is a need that you can fill.

Chapter Six Questions

1. How has social media advances affected how chaplain care is provided?

2. How are reduced hospital stays and budget cutting measures affecting the future of chaplains?

3. As the role of chaplains evolves, how might future chaplains have to adapt to remain relevant?

4. What do you think the writer meant by the following statement? "Professional standards and practice are mandatory if chaplaincy is to remain a viable and fundable endeavor."

Chapter Seven: The Conclusion

The Many Faces of Chaplaincy

Throughout this book we have been discussing the roots and origin of the chaplain ministry, the advancements of the chaplain's role in the healthcare field, and the expectations of the patients, medical professionals, and the public...of ministers in their role as chaplains. We have seen the many faces of present day chaplains; the comforter, the confidant, the counselor, the ambassador, the advocate, the one who carries with them the very presence of God.

We have traced the history and role of chaplains from bible days to present days, and beyond; with a vision for the future. The role of chaplains has evolved from caregivers to clinical professionals with standards of practice and the authority to participate in patient care planning on the interdisciplinary medical team. They serve on ethics committees helping determine the standards of practice in hospitals and other facilities providing medical care. Beyond that, they are expected to take the lead role in all things spiritual involving the medical team and the patient.

When culture and religion affect the care of the patient, the chaplain is expected to educate the medical team. This insures that the wishes of the patient are understood. The cultural and religious practices of the patient and their family need to be considered as they affect the outcome of the patient's care. The team will want to address any specific needs to insure an optimal patient recovery.

Beyond that, the chaplain is to be present for the staff just as they are for the patients. They pray for them, counsel them, and support them in any way that they can. The medical facility is the chaplain's church and the people that work and visit there are their congregation.

Chaplains may be asked to administer communion, perform baptism, or perform the memorial service of a patient when they die. We will not go into detail on how to perform these specifically. If you need further assistance on preparing to perform any of these I suggest a pastor's handbook. There are many good ones available that will offer sermon samples and the proper scriptures as are appropriate.

The Routine Day

Any day in the life of a chaplain is usually less than routine. It would be impossible to anticipate all the possible scenarios. The day may include many different duties, unexpected circumstances, or crises. Therefore, the chaplain needs to be prepared for anything.

How does one prepare for anything? It begins with having an intimate relationship with the Lord, and an active faith. Take the time to do a personal assessment of your own relationship with the Lord. Make time to be prepared in mind, body, and spirit.

In the busyness of life and career, don't forget to nurture yourself. Plenty of rest and relaxation, a healthy lifestyle, and time spent in bible study and prayer; all will carry you farther than an empty tank of gas. Before you can pour out of your abundance, you must have an abundance from which to pour. Empty vessels have little to offer to others. Before you step into the chaplain's role for the day, be prepared.

Some of the things you can anticipate in a routine day are meeting many new people for the very first time, praying and listening to the needs of patients and staff alike. Keep your eyes and ears attuned to what is being said, both verbally and in body language.

Your spiritual discernment needs to be turned up to see the clues that people are unable to verbalize. Remember the patient Mary who was described as needy? She was needy for a reason, she had just lost her husband and was unable to verbalize her loss to others.

She would reach out because it was her only method of communicating her need.

Your first visit may be the only opportunity you have to meet the patient before they leave. What are you sensing while you are present with the patient? Do they need further evaluation? Something not mentioned previously is patient confidentiality. Remember that you are obligated to keep the confidence of the patient. Legally you cannot divulge any information to anyone not authorized to have that information.

There is one important consideration, if you suspect the patient or others are in danger, such as in the case of suspected abuse; you are obligated legally to report it to the proper authorities. The report should be made to the person you report to in your role as a chaplain. Secondly, you must report it to the proper legal authorities. Abuse in any form needs to be dealt with before it escalates. You are obligated under law to report such concerns.

Next, conduct a short assessment and determine if the patient has needs that may benefit from additional assistance. If they do, then you will want to do a full assessment to determine the extent of those needs, identify appropriate goals and plan the interventions. This is the total spiritual care plan. This care plan will become a part of the overall patient care plan and you may need the whole interdisciplinary team participating in certain interventions as is appropriate.

Therefore, it is important to maintain good communication with the whole care team. The plan of care for the patient needs to be cohesive with the plans of other team members. As a team, you work together to provide the best possible care for the patient.

So, in conclusion, the routine of a typical chaplain visit includes introductions, brief preliminary assessment, potentially a full spiritual assessment and history, goals, interventions, and finally implementation of the spiritual plan of care.

The care for the patient includes care for the family, and care for the medical staff. Take the lead in all things spiritual; as the spirit leads and within the limitations imposed by the governing powers where you are employed. A typical day may lead you to a dying patient's home, to a rehab hospital, or an emergency room.

Final Thoughts

Remember the reporter interviewing the people in the street back in the beginning of this book? He asked them, what is a chaplain? The answers were varied, some did not know. If that same reporter walked up to you, what would you say?

I trust that you could give a very honest and educated summary of what we have learned. Perhaps your answer would include:

"A chaplain is someone who cares. They bear with them the presence of the Lord and become his hands and feet upon the earth, much like the good Samaritan. They come along side others in times of crisis, joining them in their journey. They assess the needs, determine the best possible goals and interventions, and implement them by God's grace. They are the shepherds of the workplace, responsible to God himself for the care they provide."

I remind you of the two greatest commandments Jesus gave us in Matthew 22:37-39

> *"You shall love the Lord your God with all your heart, with all your soul, and with all your mind. This is the greatest and foremost commandment. The second is like it, You shall love your neighbor as yourself."*

What better explanation can one give? A chaplain loves the Lord and he cares for others. Amen

To the Reader

While many reading this book will not be pursuing full-time employment as a chaplain, the concepts placed in this book give you a bird's eye view of what the work of a full-time chaplain entails. The mission and goals of chaplains in any capacity still apply as we reach out to others in need.

Even as a part-time chaplain or as a church lay leader caregiver, it is possible to fulfill the call. It is also possible to obtain financial support to fund your work. For more information on fund raising and personal coaching please contact ksmith@vision.edu.

May God bless as you endeavor to fulfill the call of God upon your life in serving others and God himself.

[24]{.small} The LORD bless you, and keep you;

[25]{.small} The LORD make His face shine on you,
And be gracious to you;

[26]{.small} The LORD lift up His countenance on you,
And give you peace.'

Numbers 6:24-26

Glossary of Terms

Term	Definition
Allied Health	"a broad field of health-care professions made up of specially trained individuals (such as physical therapists, dental hygienists, audiologists, and dietitians) who are typically licensed or certified but are not physicians, dentists, or nurses" Merriam Webster Medical Dictionary [41]
Cappella	Latin word for cloak
Holistic Medicine	"relating to or concerned with wholes or with complete systems rather than with the analysis of, treatment of, or dissection into parts <holistic medicine attempts to treat both the mind and the body." Merriam Webster Medical Dictionary[42]

[41] https://www.merriam-webster.com/medical/

[42] https://www.merriam-webster.com/medical/

Interdisciplinary Health Team	A group of health care professionals from diverse fields who work in conjunction with one another toward a common goal of patient health.
Nursing Care Plan	A nursing care plan provides direction on the type of nursing care the individual family may require. The focus of a nursing care plan is to facilitate standardized evidence-based and holistic care.
Palliative Care	"…medical and related care provided to a patient with a serious, life-threatening, or terminal illness that is not intended to provide curative treatment but rather to manage symptoms, relieve pain and discomfort, improve quality of life, and meet the emotional, social, and spiritual needs of the patient. Many still believe *palliative care* is appropriate only when nothing more can be done to treat a patient's disease and prolong life. But unlike hospice, *palliative care* can and should be delivered while patients continue treatment for their diseases." Jane E. Brody, *The New York Times*, 3 Dec. 2013
Parakletos	advocate, to come along side, to comfort

Total Patient Care	Nurse is responsible for planning, organizing, and performing ALL patient care during the assigned shift

Healthcare Assessment Sheet
for Chaplains

Belief - What is your **belief** system? Are you a person of faith and if so, what is it that you believe? What is it that gives your life meaning and purpose? How active are you in pursuing your faith?

Support - What type of personal **support system** do you have? Is your family close and available to assist you? What about your community, friends, church? Are they supportive?

Cope - How do you feel you are **coping** with your stay here? What about the diagnosis? Do you have questions or concerns? What about your family, are they having any problems dealing with your diagnosis?

Next Steps - What other problems or concerns might you have? Is there anything that I or the medical staff can assist you with during your stay here?

HEALTHCARE CHAPLAINS

Care Plan for Chaplains

Problem	Goal

INTERVENTIONS

Number each problem and designate one or more goals and interventions for each problem listed. Ex. Problem 1, Goal 1, Intervention 1a, 1 b, 1 c.

Chaplain Signature   **Date**

Bibliography

References as they appear in the footnotes of the book.

1. Professional Chaplaincy, "What is a Chaplain?", link to video https://youtu.be/QcgBmQ13dec
2. https://www.regonline.com/custImages/330000/333184/TheWorkoftheChaplainExtract.pdf
3. Drudgeon, Kate *Understanding the Whole Patient, A Model for Holistic Patient Care* June 2, 2015 of Continuum: https://www.continuuminnovation.com/en/how-we-think/blog/understanding-the-whole-patient
4. Wintz, Rev. Sue *How Chaplains Are A Valuable Part of the Health Care Team* http://www.kevinmd.com/blog/2016/03/chaplains-valuable-part-health-care-team.html
5. Holst, Lawrence E., editor, *Hospital Ministry--The Role of the Chaplain Today*, Wipf & Stock Publishers of Eugene, Oregon 2006
6. Cherny, Nathan; Fallon, Maria; Kassa, Stein; Portenoy, Russell; and Currow, David C.; authors, *Oxford Textbook of Palliative Care 5th edition* by Oxford University Press, United Kingdom 2015
7. http://enterchaplains.blogspot.com/p/3000-year-history-of-chaplaincy.html
8. http://chaplain.house.gov/chaplaincy/history.html
9. http://www.professionalchaplains.org/files/professional_standards/standards_of_practice/standards_practice_professional_chaplains_acute_care.pdf
10. http://www.professionalchaplains.org/content.asp?contentid+31 A brief history of the Association of Professional Chaplains.
11. https://docslide.net/documents/hospital-chaplains-who-needs-them.html

12. Puchalski, Christina M.; MD, MS; author *The Role of Spirituality in Health Care.* https://www.ncbi.nlm.nih.gov/pmc/articles/PMC1305900/

13. http://www.professionalchaplains.org/store_product.asp?prodid=31

14. https://youtu.be/zrCditxjyTA Video Career Profiles - Chaplain by LomaLinda360

15. Healthcare Chaplaincy; "Professional Chaplains Role"; https://youtu.be/Ox3NplKyAPI

16. Wintz, Rev. Sue, author; http://www.kevinmd.com/blog/2016/03/chaplains-valuable-part-health-care-team.html

17. https://youtu.be/zrCditxjyTA Video Career Profiles – Chaplain by LomaLinda360

18. https://youtu.be/zrCditxjyTA video Career Profiles - Chaplain by LomaLinda360

19. DeKoven, Stan E. Ph.D. author; Grief Relief; Vision Publishing, Ramona, CA 978-1931178860 http://www.booksbyvision.org

20. http://youtu.be/rwC_wgwgxXE

21. http://medical-dictionary.thefreedictionary.com/interdisciplinary+team

22. https://www.healthcarechaplaincy.org/userimages/professional-chaplaincy-its-role-and-importance-in-healthcare.pdf page 82

23. Wentz, Rev. Sue; Director, professional and community education of HCCN, author; http://www.kevinmd.com/blog/2016/03/chaplains-valuable-part-health-care-team.html

24. Pruyser, Paul W.; author; The *Minister as Diagnostician*, ISBN 0-664-24123-9 published by The Westminster Press, 1976.

25. Fitchett, George *Assessing Spiritual Needs*, A Guide for caregivers, 0-7880-9940-x published by Academic Renewal Press, Lima, Ohio 2002

26. Chaplaincy Today e-Journal of the Association of Professional Chaplains Volume 28 Number 1 Spring/Summer 2012

27. DeKoven, Stan E. Ph.D. author; Assessment in Counseling; Vision Publishing, Ramona, CA August 2010 978-1-61529-0-055; page 10. http://www.booksbyvision.org/product/assessment-in-counseling/

28. DeKoven, Stan E. Ph.D. author; Assessment in Counseling; Vision Publishing, Ramona, CA August 2010 978-1-61529-0-055; page 10. http://www.booksbyvision.org/product/assessment-in-counseling/

29. This worksheet is available in the back of your book.

30. http://www.professionalchaplains.org/files/professional_standards/standards_of_practice/standards_practice_professional_chaplains_acute_care.pdf

31. Image is public domain. https://commons.wikimedia.org/wiki/File:Maslow_hierarchy_of_needs.jpg

32. http://www.professionalchaplains.org/files/professional_standards/standards_of_practice/standards_practice_professional_chaplains_acute_care.pdf

33. https://medlineplus.gov/ency/patientinstructions/000536.htm

34. DeKoven, Stan E. Ph. D, author Grief Relief, Vision Publishing of Ramona, Ca; March 2004; www.booksbyvision.org

35. http://www.professionalchaplains.org/files/professional_standards/standards_of_practice/standards_of_practice_hospice_palliative_care.pdf

36. http://www.azquotes.com/quote/1200463

37. https://csupalliativecare.org/disability/

38. Holst, Lawrence E.; editor, Hospital Ministry, The role of the Chaplain Today, ISBN 1-59752-814-5 by Wipf and Stock Publishers, in 2006, Eugene, Oregon.

39. https://www.healthcarechaplaincy.org/news-events/entry/gaps-in-profession-still-ring-true.html

40. As previously stated, most chaplains are either part-time, volunteer, or self-funded. For more information or for coaching on how to raise funds to support your ministry please contact ksmith@vision.edu
41. https://www.merriam-webster.com/medical/
42. https://www.merriam-webster.com/medical/

Additional Resources

1. Cobb, Mark, *The Hospital Chaplain's Handbook: A Guide for Good Practice,* 1-85311-477-4/9781-85311-477-9 published by William Clawes Ltd, Beccles, Suffolk, Great Britain, 2005
2. Mack, Ronald Sr; The Basics of Hospital Chaplaincy, 1-591609-68-2; published by Xulon Press, 2003
3. Marty, Martin E. and Vaux, Kenneth L.; editors; Health/ Medicine And The Faith Traditions; 0-8006-1636-7, Fortress Press, Philadelphia, PA; 1982
4. Roberts, Rabbi Stephen B., editor; Professional Spiritual & Pastoral Care, A Practical Clergy and Chaplain's Handbook 978-1-59473-312-3 published by Skylight Paths Publishing; Woodstock Vermont; 2012

About the Author

Formerly from Ohio and North Carolina, Kathy now resides in Ramona, CA. She is an author, educator, and motivational speaker. She earned her Doctor of Ministry degree at Vision International University in 2017 and has an Associate's Degree in Nursing from Excelsior College of New York.

She is an ordained minister with the Assemblies of God International Fellowship. She works as the Communications Director for Vision International University and is the Director of Vision Publishing.

She has authored the following books:

- *Treasures of the Heart,* Gifts of the Trinity

- *Wisdom Speaks.* Hearing Her Voice in a Noisy World

- *Effective Pastoral Care Ministry* for the Local Church

- *Healthcare Chaplaincy*

Kathy teaches workshops and seminars and is available to speak on a variety of topics including, Spiritual Gifts, Anatomy of the Church, Writing Your First Book, Developing a Pastoral Care Ministry Team, and others on request.

For more information about Kathy and her ministry, you can go to www.planpurposedestiny.org or email her at ksmith@vision.edu